LEADING WITH STORY

In his introductory chapter Rick Sessoms makes the sobering observation that although 80 percent of the world's people are storycentric learners, more than 90 percent of Christian workers communicate through a highly literacy-based approach. This disconnect limits greatly the multiplication of leaders for the growing churches, but also veers from the example of Jesus himself in the preparation of leaders. He further notes how many leadership development approaches have overlooked persuasive research documenting the multiple components essential for the actual transformation of leaders. Rick Sessoms combines engaging stories from around the globe, biblical insights, current leadership research, transferable principles and practical models of effective leadership development among storycentric learners in a book that will challenge and inspire any who aspire to develop Christ-centered leaders for their own context.

David W. Bennett
chief collaboration officer and teaching pastor, *The Lausanne Movement*

From my Eastern European perspective, Rick Sessoms' statement that the "current state of Christian leadership is in despair" is very true today. Turning to Jesus' model of leadership will inevitably bring us to translate these principles and approaches into storycentric settings. Doing so, our leadership development will help people recognize their God-given roles to further develop other people and release them into serving as leaders.

Branko Bjelajac
global partner development, *TWR International*

This book on leadership by Rick Sessoms is a breakthrough response to the growing number of leaders who are ministering to oral learners, who comprise 80 percent of the world's population. This is a practical, cutting-edge book that will be of great help to them—and to all of us!

Paul Cedar
chairman, *Mission America Coalition*

It's hard to know who to trust when it comes to leadership theory and teaching. There are so many theories in the leadership market today that the collective noise tends to make the entire vertical rather repugnant. *Leading with Story* lays out a leadership model that is the closest I have seen to how Christ led his disciples and his church today that is applicable to both ministry and business. It is a surprisingly simple model but will demand everything you have within you in order to live it out. You'll have to give up your power and arrogance. You'll need to walk closely with the Lord, hear his voice, and be willing to wash another's feet. There are lots of leadership models that will help you feel better. But if you want a leadership model that is built on the person of Christ, then grab your towel. You're going to need it.

Bill English
CEO, *Mindsharp*

After a lifetime of ministry as a pastor and a seminary professor, I now wish that I could start over again with this storycentric approach to teaching and leadership. I have come to see that stories, images, and drama are more effective for life formation than abstract concepts. Of course, the storycentric approach is essential for communication in non-literate cultures. But even in the highly literate societies, effective communication has moved almost entirely to stories and images. So your work is hugely strategic for developing effective leaders in churches not only among non-literate people, but also in my own culture.

Walter Hansen
professor of New Testament, *Fuller Theological Seminary*

We live in a time when the church is growing at unprecedented rates among oral preference people. This is a book every church leader should read who takes seriously the task of reaching every tongue, tribe, and nation.

Randall Kennedy
strategy director, *The Maclellan Foundation, Inc.*

There are few leaders or organizations that are intentionally developing next-generation leaders for the future. In fact, most of the time, leader development, at any level, is the first thing to be mentioned but the last thing to be funded or significant time invested in.

Rick Sessoms takes the subject of leader development one step further and takes it into the realm of developing oral learners into effective leaders. Now that is unique! He speaks from the crucible of firsthand experience on the international leadership stage. You can smell the "smoke" of his firsthand experiences.

So let's start the journey with Sessoms as he takes us into the messy arena of preparing leaders to lead. It's hard work but the results are eternal!

Lauren Libby
president/CEO, *TWR International*

Rick Sessoms effectively uses both story and effective analysis to explain the landscape of leadership development. He goes on to provide compelling analysis that demonstrates the need for Christ-centered leaders who are willing to lead in a manner that is countercultural. The story of the towel and the basin has always been a compelling one in leadership circles. Rick again returns to this story as a key turning point for examining how Christ led and through this, his influence and impact on both leaders and organizations.

John McGee
president, *Potters Hand Consulting*

What an inspiring book! It captivates the reader with a fresh vision on how to develop and release Christ-centered Leaders who would have a lasting impact on the church that is growing by leaps and bounds, mainly in the over five billion storycentric population of our world. *Leading with Story* satisfies both the mind and the heart; it is both challenging and easy to read. The book is based on solid research and offers practical tools to rapidly multiply a new breed of leaders whose character reflects and points to the very essence of the Gospel message: Our Lord Jesus Christ! There is hope for our generation!

Jose Oliveira
West Africa Regional Leader, *United World Mission*

Everyone with a serious interest in growing leaders should read *Leading with Story*. If you are not a believer in the power of story before you read the book, you will by the time you finish! This is a timely, and wonderfully readable, book that I believe will help all of us become better leader developers.

Jane Overstreet
president/CEO, *Development Associates International*

Rick has the key to unlock a new level of communicating biblical ideals, and he provides the solid tools to make it a leadership lifestyle.

Roger Parrott
president, *Belhaven University*

Rick has an extensive and deep grasp of both issues of leadership as well as how to train those who aren't skilled in western learning methods. And . . . he has been doing just that. If you desire to raise up leaders for the next generation around the globe, this book will save you a lot of time, effort, and failed attempts to put on another translated PowerPoint seminar.

Greg Parsons
executive director, *Frontier Ventures*

When you read *Leading with Story*, you will be convinced, convicted, challenged, and compelled to improve your service to those you lead. Sessoms' inspiring work accurately describes distressing weaknesses that hinder effective leadership. Then he shows how the power of storycentric leadership development can form and empower a truly Christ-centered leader to make a positive difference in the people they serve.

Woodie J. Stevens
global discipleship director, *Church of the Nazarene*

Leading with Story is a must read for all educators regardless of location or student body. The use of storycentric presentation helps students of all ages understand and internalize concepts. Dr. Sessoms' use of examples and his own stories helps illustrate the very concepts he presents in the book.

Bruce Winston
professor of business and leadership
Regent University School of Business and Leadership

LEADING WITH STORY

CULTIVATING CHRIST-CENTERED LEADERS IN A STORYCENTRIC GENERATION

RICK SESSOMS

with Tim Brannagan

WILLIAM CAREY
LIBRARY

Published by William Carey Library
1605 E. Elizabeth St.
Pasadena, CA 91104 | www.missionbooks.org

Sharon Edwards, copyeditor
Josie Leung, graphic design
Rose Lee-Norman, indexer

William Carey Library is a ministry of
Frontier Ventures | www.frontierventures.org

Printed in the United States of America
20 19 18 17 16   5 4 3 2 1 BP300

Library of Congress Cataloging-in-Publication Data
Names: Sessoms, Richard W., author.
Title: Leading with story : cultivating Christ-centered leaders in a
    storycentric generation / Rick Sessoms.
Description: Pasadena, CA : William Carey Library, 2016. |
    Includes bibliographical references and index.
Identifiers: LCCN 2016021914 (print) | LCCN 2016023249 (ebook) |
    ISBN 9780878085309 (pbk.) | ISBN 0878085300 (pbk.) | ISBN
    9780878089895 (eBook)
Subjects: LCSH: Storytelling--Religious aspects--Christianity. |
    Christian leadership.
Classification: LCC BT83.78 .S47 2016 (print) | LCC BT83.78 (ebook) |
    DDC 253--dc23
LC record available at
    https://lccn.loc.gov/2016021914

To David Muir and Colin Buckland:

    - Christ-centered leaders.

    - Life-changing mentors.

    They finished well.

CONTENTS

Part One: Storycentric Learning

Part Two: Leadership Development

Part Three: Christ-Centered Leadership

Part Four: The Garden Project

I had a friend in college named Frank who would never wear his seatbelt. We constantly harassed him, but he would consistently ignore our warnings during the four years we were together at the university. A few years later, I was on a business trip that took me to his hometown, and Frank agreed to pick me up from the airport. After hugs and slaps on the back, we climbed into his minivan. He immediately put on his seatbelt. I was happily amazed, and playfully asked for an explanation for this new behavior. He told me of a friend of his who recently had a car crash and received forty-four stiches in his face after flying through the windshield because he was not wearing a seatbelt. As a long-time friend, I felt the freedom to ask him sarcastically, "So, you didn't know that could happen?" Frank's answer stunned me. He said, "I *knew*; I just didn't *understand*." Frank didn't gather any new information about seat belts; he simply processed old information against the back-drop of real-world (field) experience. In other words, his experience put "old information" into new relief that demanded a response.

I've always intuitively known that storytelling was a useful tool to reach nonliterate peoples. Rick Sessoms' field experiences captured in this book have put that "old information" into a new relief of *understanding* the God-sized opportunity to reach the unreached storycentric peoples of the world.

Sessoms argues here that the apologetic mode of *storytelling* is not merely an accommodation to the condition of nonliterates, but is actually preferable to the conceptual reasoning dominant in the West and in most Christian work. For example, it is part of the great hopefulness found in this book that today's millennials (largely "Western," and divorced from the institutional evangelical church) are comfortable with and eager to promote a storycentric approach to their faith. But I believe that the best argument for storytelling is that it is the preferred style of Jesus' own teaching. Therefore, the contemporary recovery of story is—not coincidentally—an opportunity to meet the global church's massive current need for effective, Christ-centered leadership.

Sessoms' work could be visited just as a handbook for biblical leadership development. He explains the limitations of the corporate, authoritarian and hierarchical style prevalent in today's leadership training, and shows that Christ-centered leadership principles lead down a strikingly different path. A return to Jesus' style of relational mentoring by established leaders can actually better impact the potential of their apprentices.

The author is careful to differentiate between the methodology of leadership development and a broader sense of an individual leader's *emergence*—the latter being primarily a function of God's work over time. Sessoms goes on to describe a comprehensive leadership "discipline" that includes character formation, biblical literacy, concept-specific skills, and ministry development—and then calls on the Church to work collaboratively to supply all of these features from its varied institutional resources.

It seems like a lot to ask from this work: both a fresh, biblical practice of leadership development and a radical re-posturing of orally-based Gospel apologetics. But these two substantial undertakings are organically connected with each other through a shared reliance on real-life, relational experience as understood through biblical examples and through a foundational understanding of how real human communication is soundly established. Thus, a storycentric preference is closest to gospel-centricity *and* most likely to produce healthy leadership in our local churches generation after generation.

This re-centering by Sessoms on story and narrative has such wide-ranging effectiveness because it is grounded in Jesus' own methods of gospel proclamation and leadership development. The one Person who is uniquely "the Truth" is the best source for universal ministry principles across time and culture and for effective witness in His name.

David Denmark
executive director, The Maclellan Foundation, Inc.

ACKNOWLEDGMENTS

The list of people and institutions that contributed to the completion of this book has been forty years in the making. Those named below also represent many others whose lives and leadership indelibly influenced my own.

Tim Brannagan, co-author, provided excellent research on story-centric learning. Tim's commitment to present ideas with clarity has made me a better writer, and his partnership in ministry has made me a better leader.

Michelle Sessoms (my first-born) applied her journalistic knack for just the right words to embroider the book's pages. She asked poignant questions and provoked a style of writing that is grounded in the real world.

John McGee sparked my thinking about a comprehensive model of leadership development. The components of leadership development in Chapter 5 are adapted from discussions with John.

Professors and coaches at Toccoa Falls College, Columbia Biblical Seminary and School of Missions, Trinity Evangelical Divinity School, and Regent University shaped my understanding of leadership and leadership development.

Colleagues who reviewed the manuscript and provided valuable recommendations for improvement include David Bennett, Steve Boone, Jim Bowman, Jason Ferenczi, Jon Hill, Matthew Smith, Greg Parsons, Woody Stephens, Tom Trageser, Bruce Winston, Felix Widmer, and Jose and France-lise Oliveira.

Leaders whose inspiring examples of Christ-centered leadership are reflected here.

Sharon Edwards and Melissa Hicks, the editorial team at William Carey Library, capably polished the initial draft into readable material.

Tina, my wife and confidant, was the force in my life to put these ideas into print. For years she said, "When are you going to write the book!" This offering is a tribute to her love and loyalty.

I'm deeply grateful to you all.

I met Chandra[1] in 2010 in New Delhi, during a seminar for Indian leaders. He had showed up at the meeting to satisfy a personal hunger for leadership growth. He also longed to know how to cultivate effective leaders for his growing ministry.

Born into a Hindu family in the state of Odisha in eastern India, Chandra had grown up without running water and electricity. Most of the people in his small village could not read or write. While training to become a Hindu priest, Chandra was miraculously converted to follow Jesus. He wanted to learn more about Jesus, so he left his village and attended a Bible college in New Delhi, many miles away from home.

At the Bible college, Chandra immersed himself in study, spending countless hours buried in theological volumes at the library and absorbing the classroom lectures like a sponge. He was a star student. After graduation Chandra was selected to teach at the college, and he eventually became a key leader of the school. But over time Chandra felt burdened to return to Odisha and minister among the people in his native village and the neighboring areas. So he resigned from his position at the Bible college and returned to the land of his childhood. Upon arrival, he wasted no time scheduling church services, preaching sermons, and teaching doctrinal truth. Surely the people would come to Jesus!

But no one responded. The people's attitudes appeared to be as hardened as the well-trodden paths in their village. Leading them to become followers of Jesus seemed impossible. What had gone wrong? Chandra became discouraged.

In 2006, Chandra was invited to a workshop that introduced him to the idea of storycentric communication. At first he was highly skeptical of this new approach, but he soon became convinced that storycentric methods of learning were more appropriate than literacy-based learning for his people. So instead of teaching them through lectures and systematic theology, he began to incorporate biblical stories, drama, and traditional music.

The results were dramatic! People responded to the storycentric methods beyond Chandra's imagination. Since 2007, the ministry he leads has planted more than 860 house churches throughout Odisha.

However, Chandra's story doesn't stop there. After the people of Odisha had responded to the gospel and house churches were launched, many congregations struggled due to the shortage of good leaders. Some of the churches even closed. Chandra realized he needed help. "How do I lead this rapidly growing network of churches?" he wondered. "How do I provide the leadership that is so crucial for these new believers and their churches? How do I develop effective, Christ-centered leaders in the storycentric villages and urban centers of Odisha?"

That is when I met Chandra in New Delhi and shared with him the principles contained in this book. Since then Chandra has grown as a leader. He has also developed other Christ-centered leaders, and his ministry has blossomed in new and exciting ways. Chandra's experience highlights a rising phenomenon among ministry leaders who are employing storycentric communication to reach people.

This phenomenon is escalating worldwide. As the Lausanne leadership team prepared for the 2010 Cape Town Congress, a global study was conducted to determine the major themes to be addressed during the meetings. This study reported—among other issues—the recent increase across the globe of conversions and church growth due to storycentric strategies. However, the report highlighted the pressing need for leadership development in story-centric communities. Something needs to be done if the church in storycentric societies is going to be healthy and reproducing. *Leading with Story* describes this acute need and offers solutions to cultivate Christ-centered, storycentric leaders.

This book addresses three factors related to Christian leaders that are hindering the healthy advance of the gospel in the twenty-first century. First, 80 percent of all the world's people—including 70 percent of Americans—are storycentric learners.[2] Some of these people must be considered storycentric learners because they are nonliterates, thus they cannot learn by any other means. But many others are storycentric because they *prefer* to learn and are most likely to be influenced through stories, images, drama, and music rather than abstract principles and conceptual thinking. While story-telling is clearly the most effective form of communication today across all cultures and contexts, more than 90 percent of Christian workers still use a literacy-based approach to communicate.

Secondly, leadership development efforts in the Christian sector generate high levels of interest and no shortage of service providers who make impressive claims of success. Yet these efforts suffer from a lack of comprehensive approaches, a scarcity of cooperation, and the virtual absence of validated effectiveness. These trends stymie the growth and limit the pool of emerging Christian leaders to serve in both the literacy-based world but particularly in storycentric communities. Using validated leadership development research, this book examines what works and what doesn't in the task of developing Christ-centered leaders.

Thirdly, Christian leaders around the world tend to practice leadership that is more akin to the predominant power leadership model of their respective cultures than the leadership example of Jesus. In Africa, church leaders often resemble tribal chiefs. In India, they typically act like gurus. North American pastors want to emulate CEOs, and Latin leaders of many Christian enterprises function like little dictators. The pattern is global, and Christian leaders in storycentric communities are not immune from these same temptations. This book provides a foundation for Christ-centered leadership in today's world.

In light of these three overlapping factors, this book intends to equip both those who provide leadership development and those who need leadership development. The following components are addressed:
- a grasp and appreciation for storycentric learning
- a comprehensive leadership development model
- an effective leadership development process
- a more precise understanding of Christ-centered leadership
- a field-tested sample of storycentric, Christ-centered leadership development

Part One examines the topic of *Storycentric Learning*, and its prominent place in our lives. This section explores the misconceptions that surround storycentric learning, the relationship of literacy and storycentric learning, and the role of story as a primary guide to living and leadership.

Part Two is about *Leadership Development*. This section unravels the confusion about leadership development that exists in the Christian community. It explains the evolution and current state of Christian leadership development, defines the comprehensive scope of leadership development that aims to cultivate Christ-centered leaders, and recommends a proven process for developing effective leaders today.

Part Three presents *Christ-centered Leadership* by outlining the trends of leadership over the past century, by explaining the current state of Christian leadership, and by proposing the need for a leadership reformation in light of the teaching and example of Christ the leader. This section explores Christ-centered leadership principles such as leading with a long view, leading with virtue, and leading others toward their potential.

Part Four describes *The Garden Project*, a pioneer leadership development initiative designed to cultivate Christ-centered leaders in storycentric communities.

Leading with Story targets several types of readers. First, the book provides guidance to mission and church leaders who are committed to raising up competent ministry leaders. A 2013 study by *Missio Nexus* gathered opinions from CEOs representing 150 ministry organizations. Those surveyed indicate that leadership development is by far the greatest perceived need / opportunity for innovation.[3] The felt need is widespread; this book offers guidelines for developing leaders who lead like Jesus in order to accelerate our Christian witness.

Second, the book is written for leadership development service providers who are looking for help in their task of cultivating emerging leaders. These individuals are asking: "What really works? What is most effective? Where do we need to be investing our energy and resources for the cause of kingdom advancement for the future?" These readers will benefit as they reflect on leadership development for storycentric learners.

Third, this book is also written for those who are interested in ministry among storycentric learners. Efforts to provide leadership development in storycentric communities are still emerging, and other fine work is being done to reach these communities for Christ. *Leading with Story* provides samples of a pioneering storycentric curriculum by Freedom to Lead International that is being used to cultivate Christ-centered leaders.

Finally, this book speaks to existing and emerging storycentric ministry leaders who are looking for a comprehensive model with a proven development process to become an effective Christ-centered leader. There is a deep longing for new generations of faithful servants of Christ who will passionately and effectively pursue the harvest. This book provides philosophical, theological, and practical guidelines to fulfill this high calling in our time.

I served on the leadership team that prepared for the Lausanne 2010 Cape Town Congress. I remember well the day in Budapest when we received the global report and heard about the rapid increase of conversions and church growth in many nations due to storycentric strategies. As Chair of Lausanne's Leadership Development Working Group, I paid close attention to the part of the report that described the great need for leadership development in storycentric communities. To put it simply, churches are growing, but leadership development was not being provided. This is where my story and Chandra's story intersect.

I have invested the majority of my ministry career coming alongside leaders with teaching, mentoring, and executive coaching, but the tools of my trade were mostly literacy-based: concepts, abstract ideas, and systems thinking. The notion of employing storycentric methods like story, images, dance, drama, and music as strategies for developing leaders had never occurred to me, even though I had been exposed to the power of story growing up in the southern United States. As a missionary teacher in Indonesia, I had even taught a seminary course on Narrative Preaching, but to be honest, I just assumed that a person had to read in order to lead. I had never stopped to consider that if this were true, then the early church would have been largely devoid of leaders since only five percent of the population was literate. Contrary to my assumptions, some of the most astounding movements in the church's 2,000-year history were led by God's storycentric servants.

The Lausanne study increased my awareness that someone needed to take on the daunting challenge of launching an initiative to cultivate Christ-centered leaders through storycentric methods. Only then could the whole gospel be unleashed in local communities. However, I struggled to reconcile my responsibility to tackle this massive need. I was not a natural candidate for the task. It would require shedding many of my own biases and accumulated expertise. It would mean laying aside much of the Western teaching philosophy that has traditionally been used to cultivate leaders. I would need to unlearn much of what I had learned; I would need to start over or at least "reboot" my teaching style. I never heard an audible voice, but in the end I sensed that God was telling me the responsibility was mine. So in 2009, I founded Freedom to Lead International (FTL).

Since meeting Chandra in 2010, I have been wrestling with the same questions he had. *Leading with Story* describes what the FTL team has learned to this point. We haven't solved all the problems. Others who follow will certainly improve upon what has been started. But this is a beginning. And this is our story.

PART ONE

Storycentric Learning

1
THE POWER OF STORY

Several years ago, my wife Tina and I visited Broadway to see the musical *Wicked*. This show, a prequel to *The Wizard of Oz*, tells the story of Elphaba, the Wicked Witch of the West, and her early history in the land of Oz. Born with an unnatural shade of green skin, Elphaba is misunderstood and ostracized. When she goes off to school, she ends up rooming with the popular Galinda, later to become The Good Witch. Galinda inspires Elphaba to travel to the Emerald City to meet the Wizard. Elphaba's only desire is to work with the Wizard, the Great and Powerful Oz. Of course, as we already know, the Wizard is not so great and powerful. He is, in fact, a fraud who turns out to be the most insidious sort of evil there is.

The matinee show we attended was packed. The story and the music were superb, and the message was riveting, filled with life lessons. Yet no one stood up at the end and said, "There are four points you ought to learn and should apply." Tina and I left with just the story stirring in our hearts and minds. We went to Starbucks and discussed it over our Caramel Macchiato and Mocha Frappuccino®.

Could it be that good and evil are often perceptions, we wondered. Is true goodness found in being true to oneself? What are the potentially negative ramifications of turning from worldly power to pursue a purer, nobler path? Powerful lessons of integrity, influence, truth, authenticity, and reconciliation were a part of our discussion. All from a musical. From a drama. From a *story*.

ENCOUNTER WITH STORYCENTRIC LEARNING

Indonesia

I was educated and trained in the United States, so reason and logic dominated my approach to vocational ministry. My initial interaction with storycentric learners occurred in 1984, when my family served as missionaries in Indonesia. My first assignment was to teach in our denomination's seminary. Since we were the new kids in town, we were assigned the courses no one else wanted to teach—one of which happened to be preaching. At least it was a course I thought I knew something about.

I taught sermon preparation in the school while listening to Indonesians preach in the local church. The church we attended was filled mostly with professional, educated Indonesians. The vast majority of our church was literate. Most of the students from the seminary went to this church. The pastor's sermons week to week were a lot like ones I'd heard and given in the US: he would present important truths intended to change how people think and how they make decisions. The sermons contained solid biblical precepts presented in several points. Sometimes he would sprinkle in a couple of quotes or illustrations for good measure.

The trouble was, the sermons in the church weren't doing much for the people in the community. There seemed to be little growth and change in how our people lived out their faith or how they reached out to others for Christ.

I noticed a different style of communication when I attended Indonesian social events. Whenever community leaders wanted to relay important information to their people, they used stories. As afternoon turned to evening and as the sun was setting, the village leaders would bring out an old bedsheet and hang it between two poles. A light was placed behind the sheet. The storyteller would use the backlit shadow of leather *wayang* puppets to create a drama.

In the darkness of night, the puppets and the stories came to life. The people—children and adults—would sit and watch and listen and laugh and learn for hours together. These puppets and their stories impacted people in ways that three-point sermons could not. The *wayang* theater reached the people's hearts. The stories they told were personal and memorable.

During that same time period, I listened to a recorded lecture series by Dr. Fred Craddock on "Preaching as Storytelling."[1] In 1996, *Newsweek Magazine* recognized Craddock as one of America's best preachers—partly because he is a master storyteller. In his Princeton lectures, Craddock posed a question: "Is there room for the story to serve as a major vehicle for communicating truth?" His question intrigued me.

I thought I would try it out. When I was asked to preach at our local Indonesian church, I took a cue from the culture and from Craddock and decided to experiment with story. I related biblical truth through a story about a man who died and entered the afterlife. The reaction from the congregation was totally unexpected—dozens responded to Christ! This was a formal church that was not accustomed to outward expression, and the Indonesian leaders' reaction was also totally unexpected. They said my presentation wasn't preaching, and it wasn't "how we do things here." They had learned well from the missionaries before me.

About a year later, the elders asked me to preach again, and again I told a story. This time I relayed the life of Caleb from the Old Testament book of Joshua. I told of how Caleb had made good choices as a young man and his choices prepared him for great things in his later years. I simply told the Scripture-based story, and not even very well. Again the people responded in extraordinary ways. As I closed the service in prayer, one man stood, raised both hands, and ran to the altar. Many others followed. All responding to God's grace served up in a story.

That was my first conscious awareness of storycentric learning. It was my first taste of the power of story as an adult. As a child, I grew up in a culture of storytellers. My father, who was an accountant, loved to tell me stories—many of the same ones his father had told *him*. The preachers of my childhood were also storytellers. In the South, where I was raised, preachers would preach to the poor, sitting on folding chairs, under tents, on floors of sawdust in wheat fields. By the power of their stories, the whole scene was changed. The streets were paved with gold. There was pearl and chandaliers all around. We were transported in space and time. God's truth served up in a story.

I didn't know much about the power of storycentric learning back then; I had only experienced it. What made me keenly aware of storycentric learning occurred years later within the Lausanne Movement.

The Lausanne Movement

The Lausanne Committee for World Evangelization, more commonly known as the Lausanne Movement, is a global network that mobilizes evangelical leaders to collaborate for world evangelization. The stated vision is "the whole church taking the whole gospel to the whole world." This is a great goal.

I served on the Lausanne leadership team. As we were preparing for the Lausanne 2010 Cape Town Congress, a study was commissioned to identify the key needs of the global church. This study uncovered a lack of substantial leadership development for ministry leaders among the majority of the world's people; those who learn best through a storycentric approach were not engaged. As Chair of the Leadership Development Working Group, I was troubled by this study.

Soon thereafter Freedom to Lead International (FTL) was launched to address this need. FTL cultivates Christ-centered leaders through story, symbol, and song to unleash the whole gospel in local communities. We seek to influence storycentric learners with the leadership principles and practices of Jesus. Part Four provides more explanation of FTL's work, but let me first tell you another part of my story.

Madhupur

Soon after the launch of FTL, I travelled to Madhupur in northeast India. This is the home of the Santali tribe, a people group of approximately eight million in which the predominant religion is Hinduism. My host for this trip was Samir, founder of a church-planting ministry among the Santalis. Samir's ministry has established a strong beachhead of churches. During my visit, I observed Samir and his colleague, Gautam, teach one of Freedom to Lead's storycentric modules entitled "Leadership for a Healthy Ministry" to eighteen of the Santali church leaders. All of these leaders are either semi-literate or nonliterate. As Samir and Gautam taught the leadership principles, they used biblical stories, as well as complementary stories, art, and music from their culture. The participants did not take notes, but they engaged deeply with the lessons by listening, drawing pictures, writing indigenous songs, creating dramas, and dancing for hours during our days together. When a Scripture reference was mentioned, one of the participants often quoted the passage from memory.

As our time together drew to a close, Samir led a debriefing session. He asked the Santali participants to recall what they had learned. One by one they shared. I was astounded as these leaders recalled the leadership principles from the module. They had grasped the lessons more accurately and more comprehensively than any literate group I had ever taught! All from pictures, music, dance, and story.

Like the Santali leaders, most of the world's people today prefer storycentric learning. Yet many of us, like my educated colleagues in Indonesia who were trained with an analytical, abstract approach, have an unfounded skepticism to the idea of story communicating the more important truths.

MISCONCEPTIONS OF STORY

Common misconceptions prevent many from considering story as a viable means of communicating truth. Story in many people's minds conveys images of fairytales or children's time at the local library. It is perceived as "just for fun" and "just for kids." We will make an exception for C. S. Lewis's *The Chronicles of Narnia*, J. R. R. Tolkien's *The Lord of the Rings*, or any number of classic myths, but for the most part, stories are for children.

Story also suffers from a bad reputation. In business, politics, and even in the church, it is assumed that story is used to put a spin on something. It is seen as a ploy to stretch logic; certainly not a vehicle to convey deeper, more serious thought. Moreover, for many the word "story" is not just a light word, it is a *negative* word. It means *untrue*.

As a child, I would say to my grandmother, "I must have lost the change. It was in my pocket when I left the store." To which she would say, "Now, son, don't you tell me a story." With this negative view of story, Craddock's question rings in my ear: *Is there room for the story to serve as a major vehicle for communicating truth?*" Some doubt it.

But have our preconceived notions about story caused us to dismiss one of the most powerful communication and teaching tools available? Could it be that story can reach into the hearts and minds of learners and teach them concepts, beliefs, values, attitudes, and facts where other approaches have had difficulty? *Yes!* Story can be invaluable in sharing the gospel as well as teaching the conceptual principles and practices of Christ-centered leadership development.

A Dictionary Difficulty

We tend to grasp the meaning of words or concepts by viewing or defining them in association to their opposite. We understand one word better when comparing it to its antonym. For example, the word *hot* takes on additional meaning when compared to *cold*. More meaning is given to *high* when compared to *low*. Compared to *poor*, the word *rich* takes on relative meaning. But the English language has no antonym for *story* apart from *non-story*. And without thought, story is then related to other similar *non* comparisons: fiction versus nonfiction (fact); truth versus non-truth (lies); real versus unreal (fantasy). Thus, story is often equated with make-believe, unreality, and fiction.

Just as my grandmother thought that my "losing the change" was just a "story," people often use the term "story" to refer to communication that is not true. The comment is heard from the classroom to the halls of Congress: "Why didn't she just tell us the facts?" "Is he trying to cover up something and put a positive spin with a story?" Stories are generally assumed to contain untruths or at best half-truths.

Of course, the content contained in a story may be true or false, imagined or validated. Whether the content is fact or fiction, the use of the term *story* here refers to a way of structuring the information for the sake of learning and meaning. Story is a type of scaffolding on which any content can be placed.

An Educational Difficulty

We are usually introduced to stories as children. Most of these childhood stories are fictional, designed to entertain or educate. However, as we grow up, we are taught to put away these childish things. While stories can illustrate and highlight important information, we are encouraged to grow out of the story realm and enter the adult world of non-story facts.

With that idea echoing in the mind, some find it difficult to use story as a vehicle for communicating the truth of the gospel. Story just doesn't seem serious enough. When a listener evaluates the speaker and says, "Well, he told some good stories," it is often another way of saying, "There was no substance to it." Story is often seen as "lightweight," particularly in the grown-up spiritual realm. Most Bible colleges and seminaries teach abstract, analytical, systematic communication styles. And that is what we come to expect pastors and teachers to present.

Institutions of higher education have created a prejudice in us against story. In college we prepare papers and reports that are graded upon their analytical content. Due largely to the Western education model, story is considered fringe, embroidery, or decorative edge. In a conversation with one pastor about the use of story, I was told: "The truth is too important. I can't just rely on the story. I have to underline this. I have to make it clear so that everybody understands it." And how does this pastor do that? To show that the truth is really important, most of the time he dismisses the story—it might be interesting, but it cannot carry the freight after all—and he replaces the story with exhortation. He fills the air with "ought" and "must" and "should." He abandons the story, and resorts to guilt and pressure in an effort to solicit the desired effects. Perhaps this explains why many listeners, even in the literacy-based world, find church teaching hard to listen to. Appropriate exhortation has its place, yet some preachers never quite get the point when somebody says, "You know, I remember that story you told in your sermon from ten years ago."

No matter how much education we have, no matter how old we are, stories still move us. They connect us. They change us. In story-centric cultures, both in the West and elsewhere, stories are not just decorative embroidery. From a biblical perspective, the story doesn't just illustrate the gospel; the story *carries* the gospel.

Story can carry higher levels of learning, too. It can create context and relevance for complex concepts, attitudes, facts, and information to be passed on. Story can help change the motivation and values of the listener. Through story, information can be easier to recall and use. Story can have far-reaching impact and influence.

THE IMPACT OF STORY

What is Story?

Story has great power to influence people. But story also suffers from misconceptions. So let's clear the confusion by clarifying the terms. When I talk about story, I am refering to a communication structure that is character-based and is driven by details that describe the character's motives, obstacles, and struggles to reach a goal. In an effective story, events happen not for their own sake, but to explain human struggle. In this context, story can then trigger and drive our thinking to understanding, meaning, and relevance.

The Bible is story—it is the Grand Narrative. The vast majority of the Word of God is narrative and can be taught in story form. Even Paul's New Testament epistles are didactic reflections on his own story. It is true that portions of the Bible are more abstract in nature and these sections must also be communicated. But I wonder if we have pushed the abstract, linear, systematic approach to learning too far too fast to the exclusion of a natural storycentric approach. We will return to this topic in a later section.

Can Adults Learn Through Story?

Will adults listen to stories? Yes, as readily as children. And not only do adults listen to story, but all of us learn from story as well. Storyteller and researcher Kendall Haven examined thousands of pages of research across fifteen fields including the cognitive sciences, neurological sciences, and developmental psychology. He also collected anecdotal evidence from thousands of educators and businesses. Through his research he made the conclusion that everyone learns from stories.[2] Not a single piece of evidence contradicted the premise that stories are universally effective and efficient for teaching and learning.

While it is true that some of us do learn best by abstract propositions presented in lectures and outlines, all of us learn through story. Most people around the world, including a growing population in the West, do not learn well through abstract concepts. They prefer to learn through story. If we want our hearers to absorb truth, then why not teach in a way that most people in the world are enthusiastic about? A storycentric approach, with truth woven in the midst of character, challenge, and purpose, helps everybody learn, even the most educated.

How Story Impacts Our World

Let's look at a couple of examples to see how the power of story impacts people.

Designated Driver

In the 1980s, Jay Winsten, a professor at Harvard, learned about the "designated driver" norm that was prevalent in Scandinavian countries. At the time the norm did not exist in the United States. Nobody knew what a designated driver was. In 1991, three years after Winsten launched his "Designated Driver" campaign, 90 percent of Americans were familiar with the term. Of those polled, 37 percent said they had acted as a designated driver, and 54 percent of frequent drinkers indicated that they had been driven home by a designated driver. How did Winsten do that? What was his secret? Winsten did not start by writing a reasoned treatise on the perils of drunk driving. Nor did he debate with senators in an attempt to enact new laws. Rather, he used story. Winsten seeded the new idea by collaborating with producers, actors, and writers from more than 160 prime-time TV programs in Hollywood to naturally insert designated-driver moments into plots. He always requested "just five seconds" of dialogue featuring the designated-driver idea.

Segments featuring the designated driver appeared on shows like *Mr. Belvedere* and *Who's the Boss*. A designated-driver poster also appeared on *Cheers*. In one episode of the 1990s hit series *LA Law*, the show's star asked the bartender to call his designated driver.

Winsten's strategy paid off. The behavior contagion among Americans to designate drivers was credited for a decrease of alcohol-related traffic fatalities from 24,000 in 1988 to 18,000 in 1992—a 25 percent reduction in just three years, and it was accomplished through story.[3]

Combating Heart Disease

Heart disease affects millions of people and consumes billions of dollars of health care each year. The lifestyle choice of excessive smoking, drinking, eating, and inadequate exercise all contribute to this crisis. For decades the medical industry has tried to address this health and financial problem.

The traditional approach has been relatively straightforward. Factual information is given about healthier life choices. Patients are told that they must eat better and get more exercise or else they will soon face death. Conventional wisdom suggests that such a life-or-death crisis should be a powerful motivator. But it isn't.

Dr. Edward Miller, former dean of Johns Hopkins University Medical School, said that when you look at people two years after heart surgery, 90 percent of them have not changed their lifestyle. He says people know they have a potentially fatal disease and that they should change how they live, but for whatever reason 90 percent do not or cannot.[4]

However, Dr. Dean Ornish, founder of the Preventative Medical Research Institute, has found a way to bring effective change to heart patients. It includes story. Realizing that providing healthcare information alone is not sufficient, Dr. Ornish inspires his patients to imagine their lives as healthier people. He helps them to picture how they can enjoy life, family, and friends without pain and with good health. It has made a huge difference. Rather than just 10 percent changing their lives with the conventional approach, Ornish has found that 77 percent of his patients stick to their lifestyle changes. His patients have a renewed outlook and a new life story.[5]

These examples show that story can have great power in how we learn and how we live. Story can really affect our faith and our leadership. In the next chapters we will see that people rely on both rational thinking and experiential learning to make sense of life. And story is at the heart of both.

CHAPTER 1 SUMMARY

- Story has power across cultures to change the minds and hearts of people.
- Story suffers from misconceptions due to its association with fairy tales, fiction, and "lightweight" communication.
- The term *story* is a way of structuring information for the sake of learning and meaning. It is character-based and driven by details and events that happen in order to explain human struggle.
- Modern education has created a bias against story; however, research indicates that learning is actually enhanced through story.
- Examples demonstrate how story has a significant impact on human behavior.

2
LITERACY AND STORY

Literacy is something to be celebrated. The ability to read and write has powerful effects on one's life. These fundamental skills provide individuals with the freedom to understand the world, to lead an informed life, to communicate with others, and to be in touch with what is going on. A good education opens up a world of opportunities and privileges that the uneducated masses do not enjoy. Any educated person who does not commit to the basic education of others is acting irresponsibly.

However, literacy has a dark side. Those of us who have grown up in highly literate societies tend to think that our ways of learning and communication are superior to storycentric cultures. When this faulty thinking persists, it distorts our worldview, erodes the perceived need for story in our own lives, and leads us to underestimate the intelligence and abilities of a majority of the world's people.

This chapter explores the benefits and liabilities of literacy. I will also present the essential value of storycentric learning to enhance literacy among people everywhere.

THE BENEFITS OF LITERACY

In 1439, Johann Gutenberg was tinkering around with an old winepress and adapted it to become the first movable-type printing press. His invention lit the fuse on a reading revolution. The wide distribution of ideas became possible for the first time in human history, and the mass production of books made it harder to suppress the flow of thought among common people. Printing led to a higher degree of accuracy and standardization of texts. The decrease in the cost of books made it possible for people to learn outside the traditional educational system. In short, reading and writing came within the reach of common people. It fueled the rapid acceleration of higher order thinking and led to unprecedented intellectual development. This has been an extraordinary gift to people and societies. The advance of both Western culture and the church over the past 575 years is due in no small part to literacy. No wonder *Time Magazine* named Gutenberg the "man of the millennium."[1] In this new millennium, where so much depends on writing, literacy continues to liberate people, and benefits them in a variety of ways.

Quality of Life

Literacy can play a major role in tackling public health problems. Basic education can develop an individual's capacity to be informed, and can generate social understanding in ways that may be extremely important in facing critical health issues. Basic education tends to facilitate the implementation of public health measures, such as immunization, sanitation, or the prevention of epidemics. On the contrary, lack of basic education creates the potential for tragic health conditions. For example, a friend described a village in Africa where many of the children were born blind. The village midwives believed it was bad for a pregnant woman to eat eggs, which contain a necessary vitamin for eyesight. Jean Drèze and Amartya Sen cite another example among nonliterate families in Uttar Pradesh, India. A study found that half of the children were undernourished; yet 94 percent of the mothers described their child's nutritional status as "normal." There is powerful evidence of a close relationship between family literacy and children's health and survival in many countries.[2] Basic education and literacy can significantly reduce these misperceptions, and they tend to reduce the public health problems.

The schooling of young women can substantially enhance their voice in family decisions. For instance, young women's education tends to have a strong downward impact on fertility rates. Those whose lives are most affected by the frequent bearing and rearing of children are young women; therefore, education enhances their voice to prevent over-frequent childbearing.

Economic Opportunity

Economic opportunities and employment prospects often depend on a person's educational achievements and cultivated skills. The ability to understand written information and to keep track of the numbers involved in particular tasks can be necessary qualifications for even simple jobs.

In addition, participation in a globalized economy is difficult to accomplish if a population cannot read and write. The success of economies like China has been based substantially on the ability of a reasonably well-educated workforce to meet the demands of quality control and skill formation involved in producing goods and services. This is a lesson that societies in Africa and South America are also learning.

Political Voice and Social Security

Literacy also enhances the political voice of people and thus contributes directly to their security and safety. It is certainly possible for people's collective voice to be heard even while they are still nonliterate; but the reach of that voice will be much greater when they are socially empowered with the ability to read newspapers, periodicals, and books, and to use written means to communicate with others at a distance. For example, the Reformers employed the written word to challenge the corruption and abuse of the medieval Catholic Church, which would not have happened without the rise of literacy among the masses. The people's ability to read for themselves what Scripture said gave traction to Martin Luther's cause.

Legal Rights

Education makes a difference to the understanding and use of legal rights—the legislated rights that people already have. Often nonliterate people cannot access or utilize their rights because they do not know about those rights. When people cannot read and write, their ability to comprehend and invoke their legal rights is severely limited. By the same token, education can significantly contribute to reducing social inequalities.

Learning is a Liberating Activity

Learning is a liberating activity in and of itself. If good learning is available and supported, then the very process of schooling can augment the quality of life for people, quite apart from the long-term benefits they receive from it. Schooling is greatly preferable to child labor, domestic work, or other more extreme alternatives. Learning can make the lives of people fun in the short-term as well as rewarding in the long-term.

There is an undeniable link between basic education and the welfare of individuals and communities. From a societal perspective, the provision of quality public education in North America and parts of Europe was a major factor in the extraordinary social development as well as the economic prosperity of the twentieth century. These lessons have also inspired Asia's rising economic powers. The transforming role of public education was seen with remarkable clarity first in Japan and later in South Korea, Taiwan, Singapore, and Hong Kong. Mainland China, too, has followed a similar route by firmly focusing on basic education and literacy.

Reading, writing, and arithmetic empower people with greater capacity to enhance their personal lives, their families, their communities, and their nations. A comprehensive strategy for servicing non-literate learners may begin with a storycentric approach, but it also encourages literacy and basic education for all. And as we will see, a storycentric approach by its very nature can propel and promote literacy within communities, in addition to the benefits of the whole gospel.

THE "DARK SIDE" OF LITERACY

However, there is a dark side to literacy. If pushed too far, literacy with its focus on the intellect has a tendency to diminish the perceived value of our heart and emotions as pesky little distractions. The unintended outcome of literacy-driven rationalism is that people have been conditioned to overuse one hemisphere of the brain over the other.

The topic of the difference between the two hemispheres of the brain – the right hemisphere and the left hemisphere - has fascinated people for thousands of years. Discussions about the similarities and differences between the brain's two hemispheres are in no short supply. In comparing two computers, for example, it is true that there are far greater similarities between a Mac and a PC as a whole than there are differences between, say, their microprocessors. From this perspective, Iain McGilchrist, a researcher in neuroimaging at Johns Hopkins University, reasserts that both hemispheres seem to be involved in one way or another in almost everything we do; however, he also shows a fundamental difference between the hemispheres regarding the type of attention they give to the world.[3]

McGilchrist demonstrated that the two hemispheres are "asymmetrical"; that is, they specialize in different functions. Whereas the right hemisphere is attuned to the apprehension of new input from one's environment, the left tends to see things abstracted from context. The two hemispheres are intended to function in a back and forth "reverberative" fashion. In other words, the left hemisphere is supposed to respond to outside signals received by the right hemisphere to create logical categories that make sense out of life. In turn, the right hemisphere provides further real-time input through sensory experience and intuition (story) that continually adjusts the left hemisphere's conceptual frameworks. The brain functions at its best when the two hemispheres are collaborating and cooperating. Without the left hemisphere, we could live like animals without being able to pause and consider. Without the right hemisphere, we can float off like an observing eye, detached from the real world around us.

My Left Brain is a Bully

McGilchrist makes the case that all previous societies started with experience (a right hemisphere function) and moved to abstract reasoning (a left hemisphere function). However, Descartes and the Enlightenment—or what is called modernity—tragically shifted the starting point in our thinking. Despite all their contributions, Enlightenment scholars had a preference for rational thinking (left hemisphere) and were suspicious of experience (right hemisphere). Modernists put excessive and misplaced rationality before metaphor, so the West eventually became a lead-with-the left culture.

That's a problem. According to McGilchrist, the left hemisphere often overshadows the right hemisphere, and operates as though it is bringing things about entirely on its own with sophisticated language and concepts. In other words, the left ultimately says to the right, "Who needs you?" This rational, analytical left hemisphere of our brain is a bully.

My friend Mike Metzger of The Clapham Institute claims there is an even bigger dilemma; It is only in the "right brain" that we experience the world as it truly is. The left merely explains experience, creating meaningful categories from the real world. But acting on its own, the left hemisphere becomes unaware. Cut off from the right hemisphere and fresh experiences, the left learns nothing new. It just keeps recycling old information. Yet as Mike says, "If your head never tilts, your mind never changes."[4] The problem becomes acute when a lead-with-the-left society becomes trapped in the left-hemisphere, literacy-based, superficial world.

McGilchrist explains the "left brain" dilemma through a story from Nietzsche that goes something like this.[5] There was once a wise spiritual master who was the ruler of a small but prosperous domain. He was known for his selfless devotion to his people. As his people flourished and grew in number, the bounds of this small domain spread. This growth also increased the master's need to implicitly trust the emissaries he sent to ensure the safety of the land's more distant parts. It was not possible for him personally to order all that needed to be dealt with. Therefore, the spiritual master began nurturing and carefully training his emissaries in order that they could be trusted. Eventually, however, there was one emissary who was more clever and ambitious than all the others, which just so happened to be the one that the master most trusted to do his work. As a result, rather than continuing his role as an emissary, he began to see himself as the master and used his position to advance his own wealth and influence. This emissary started to view his spiritual master's temperance and forbearance as weakness rather than wisdom, and on his missions on the master's behalf he adopted the mantle as his own. The emissary soon became contemptuous of his master. And so it came about that the master was usurped, the domain became a tyranny, and eventually the kingdom collapsed in ruins.

This story illustrates something taking place inside ourselves, inside our very brains. This drama has been playing out over the last 500 years or so since the invention of the printing press. Though the cerebral hemispheres should cooperate, they are in a state of conflict. The subsequent battles between them are recorded in the history of Western culture. At present our civilization finds itself in the hands of the emissary. The Master, the one whose wisdom gave the people peace and security, has been betrayed by the emissary. Our left brain preference has restructured our worldview, made efficiency king, created suspicion toward feelings, and caused us to overlook capable leaders.

A Restructured Worldview

Learning to read and write actually restructures our worldview. To illustrate, author Shane Hipps writes about teaching his daughter "The ABC Song":

> We introduced her to one of the most powerful technologies the world has ever known . . . the technology of letters , the invention of writing. In a way, teaching her how to read was actually teaching her brain to do something completely unnatural. The skills of walking and talking arrived intuitively over time, but reading and writing forced her brain to operate in a way that was not innate. She had to learn to compress reality into line after line of strange shapes arranged in sequence. Such a technology takes work to master and, when mastered, completely transforms our consciousness.[6]

Marshall McLuhan, the futurist who made famous his idea that "the medium is the message," also points out that the broad introduction of literacy into our culture has altered the way people think.[7] McLuhan maintains that the introduction of literacy has restructured the worldview of entire civilizations. In other words, our thinking patterns actually mirror the things we use to think with. For instance, the printing press was the first assembly line, the archetype for nearly every kind of mechanization that followed. The efficient, linear, sequential form of printing helped make possible the Industrial Revolution and the subsequent methods of mass production to make everything from nickels to Nissans. Literacy also changed architecture; for example, the linear arrangement of pews in churches did not exist before the printing press was invented. After printing began, church seating was constructed in rows to mirror the page of a book.[8]

Efficiency Becomes King

When linear reasoning prevails, efficiency becomes preeminent. In a world where the left brain is in charge, our packaging of the gospel has been compressed for efficiency. Printing has led to restructuring our imagination and our belief systems. The Bible presents redemptive history as a four-part drama—creation, fall, redemption, and restoration. Yet the advent of literacy has even reshaped the gospel. Hipps asserts this when he writes,

> Under the force of the printed word, the gospel message was efficiently compressed into a linear sequential formula:

> Confess your Sins + Believe in Jesus = Go to Heaven

> Such a stunning compression of the gospel, from four-part drama to essentially a two-part play (fall and redemption) would not have been possible prior to the age of the printed word and literacy.[9]

Medieval cathedrals told the story of the Bible in elaborate stained-glass windows. They presented people with a vast array of images that represented the grand sweep of biblical narrative. The message was far from distilled—and simplified—as it is today in literacy-based cultures. As Hipps says, "Printing makes us prefer cognitive modes of processing while at the same time atrophying our appreciation for mysticism, intuition, and emotion. It can even make us suspicious or fearful of feelings, especially as they interact with our 'logical' faith."[10]

Suspicious of Feelings

A literacy-based mindset also tends to undermine the primary role of feelings in our decisions and behavior. This is well illustrated by "The Four Spiritual Laws," an evangelistic tract by the late Bill Bright. The impact of Bill Bright and Campus Crusade upon the planet is noteworthy. Many of us have memorized and used "The Four Spiritual Laws" in evangelistic efforts with others. These "Laws" go something like this: (1) God loves you and offers a wonderful plan for your life; (2) People are sinful and separated from God. Therefore, we cannot know and experience God's love and plan for our lives; (3) Jesus Christ is God's only provision for man's sin. Through Him you can know and experience God's love and plan for your life; and (4) We must individually receive Jesus Christ as Savior and Lord. Then we can know and experience God's love and plan for our lives. These "Laws" are a logical, efficient presentation of the gospel.

Bright declared that this message is accepted through reason. Then his message goes farther. Toward the back of the little pamphlet, Bright issues a stark warning under the heading "Do Not Depend on Feelings." What follows is a well-known train diagram and explanation.

According to the graphic, the train has three main cars: the engine, a boxcar, and the caboose. The engine represents the facts of the gospel—"The Four Spiritual Laws." The boxcar is labeled "faith," indicating faith follows the facts. Finally, the caboose is named "feeling" with the indication that the train will run with or without the caboose. In the same way, Christians are instructed not to depend on feelings or emotions, but we are to place our reasoned faith in God's promise given to us in His Word.

This graphic is partly right. Faith in the reality of the gospel is critical. But the graphic minimizes the essential role of feelings in making life's most important decisions. This is a typical problem with a highly literate approach to spirituality. For a generation of Western believers, this model has predominated our perception of the proper way of presenting and responding to the gospel. Feelings are more than just sweaty palms and tearful eyes. Feelings include hope, joy, compassion, grief, and peacefulness. These are necessary emotions that impact our heart and soul, feelings we can ill afford to lose. They are integral to the Christian life.

Some notable writers speak of the place of emotion in the Christian experience. C. S. Lewis, for example, famously stated,

> It would seem that Our Lord finds our desires not too strong, but too weak. We are half-hearted creatures, fooling about with drink and sex and ambition when infinite joy is offered us, like an ignorant child who wants to go on making mud pies in a slum because he cannot imagine what is meant by the offer of a holiday at the sea. We are far too easily pleased.[11]

John Piper also recognizes the important role of emotions for Christian faith and living. In his book *Desiring God*, Piper reflects on the Westminster Catechism's opening words: "The chief end of man is to glorify God and enjoy Him forever." He proposes that there is no distinction between glorifying God and enjoying him, and suggests that those familiar words could read, "The chief end of man is to glorify God BY enjoying Him forever."[12] The role of feelings is vital in the journey of faith.

Lesslie Newbigin believed that a rational, efficient approach to the gospel has malformed the church. Newbigin recognized this malady while working as a missionary in India for over thirty years. He wrote, "The churches of Europe and their cultural offshoots in the Americas have largely come to a kind of comfortable cohabitation with the Enlightenment."[13]

This rational, efficient approach hinders the church's effectiveness among 80 percent of the world's people, including over 70 percent of the U.S. population who are storycentric learners.[14] These intelligent storycentric learners are most influenced when communication comes in a story structure. They prefer to transmit their beliefs, heritage, values, and other important information by means of stories, proverbs, poetry, music, dance, drama, and ceremony. While postmodern secularists accommodate storycentric learners by using metaphor—stories from experience, images, music, and the like—to win people over, most church leaders still do not. D. A. Carson, a professor at Trinity Evangelical Divinity School, points out that most Western discipleship methods are merely subsets of systematic theology, thus the good news of Jesus Christ is virtually incoherent to most of our listening world.[15] Evangelical leaders have been heavily influenced by modernity, so they prioritize the use of logic and efficiency to make their biblical case.

As Christian leaders we often communicate the Bible in the same way that it was modeled to us. But our default method may not be as effective in the storycentric world as we assume. During a professional gathering several years ago, a number of Western presenters talked of their success in crafting and communicating Bible stories in various parts of the world. After half a dozen or more had lauded their accomplishments, an Ethiopian man named Berhanu stood up and shared his story. He was born into an animistic, Islamic tribe in Southern Ethiopia, and had heard the gospel as a teenager. He began to follow Jesus, but remained a secret believer. In due course, Berhanu had the opportunity to travel abroad for education. It was his heart's desire to reach his people, but he then told the sad story of how he was no longer effective among his own people because of his Western teaching style. His people considered him an outsider. His literacy-based education had rendered Berhanu unable to communicate with his own people! He concluded by challenging us to consider whether Westerners are really as effective as we give ourselves credit for.

Christian workers from highly literate societies have learned ways of communication that have limited effectiveness among many of the people they are attempting to reach. Oftentimes it is not resistance to the message as much as it is resistance to our teaching preference. Preaching our three-point homilies and teaching abstract doctrine (left hemisphere) trump experiencing the gospel (right hemisphere). We just replay the familiar. Paradigms are never challenged. Faith is never unsettled. Idols are never upended. Our sermons convince only the already-convinced. Real-life messiness is solved in thirty minutes.

This Enlightenment preference for left hemisphere over right hemisphere has impacted the way most Christians engage with church every week. We attend services and attend Bible studies that are dominated by words—concepts and theology and "ancient truths"—that may not have much connection with life. Mike Metzger maintains that the most damaging effect of suppressing the heart is that it deadens desire.[16] Today, many people feel exiled from modernist religious expressions that are leading with the left and are forever rehearsing the familiar. The faith of many has grown stale. But we are not just intellectual creatures. Our emotional life is integral to our very being and our relational life with God.

Overlooked Leaders

From the time of the Gutenberg Bible, Christianity has "walked on literate feet."[17] With all of its attending advantages, literacy has also *hindered* access to the gospel message itself. While the vast majority of the world's unreached people are storycentric, an estimated 90 percent of the world's Christian workers present the truth using expositional, analytical, abstract, logical communication. With this bias toward the presentation of truth, we expect the rest of the world to adjust to our way of communication and jump through our hoops. Moreover, we expect ministry leaders to be able to learn and to communicate in our analytical, abstract ways as well.

The Kasena people in northern Ghana are storycentric learners who primarily practice folk Islam. Years ago a number of the people in one Kasena village came to faith in Jesus through Kaba, a local believer. Sometime later, foreign missionaries came to the village with the *Jesus Film*, seeking to establish a church and to look for spiritual leaders. Kaba was overlooked because he was not literate. One of Kaba's converts, a young man named Kwotua, tells it this way:

> I was a child in an idol-worshipping home when my spiritual father, Kaba, took an interest in me. He spoke with me, encouraged me, and guided me more than any other person. Kaba mentored me and many others of our village. But Kaba was never identified as a leader because he could not read. He tried three times to pass the literacy exam, but failed. Kaba's prayer was that, although he could not be a Christian leader on earth, the Lord would ordain him in heaven.[18]

Leaders like Kaba possess the intelligence, the capacity, and the trust of their communities to serve as recognized Christ-centered leaders. A fundamental shift must take place in our thinking for the sake of kingdom advancement worldwide.

One-Eyed Prophets

When dealing with the "dark side" of literacy, we are faced with the reality that our left brain often wants to suppress the right brain. We have seen how learning to read and write actually causes a restructuring of worldview: it leads us to become servants of efficiency, to become suspicious of feelings, and to have a tendency to overlook those with real potential for leadership simply because they are not literacy-based learners. Combine all this together, and we are in danger of becoming one-eyed prophets.

Thousands of years ago, Socrates taught one of his pupils about two Egyptian gods: a king named Thamus and an inventor named Theuth, who was known to have invented geometry, arithmetic, astronomy, and writing. Socrates told the story:

> Now the king of all Egypt at that time was the god Thamus. . . . To him came Theuth to show his inventions, saying that they ought to be imparted to the other Egyptians. . . . When it came to writing, Theuth declared, ". . . I have discovered a sure receipt for memory and wisdom." To this Thamus replied, ". . . you have attributed to it quite the opposite of its real function. Those who acquire it will cease to exercise their memory and become forgetful. . . . What you have discovered is a receipt for recollection, not for memory. And as for wisdom, your pupils will have the reputation for it without the reality; they will receive a quantity of information without proper instruction. . . . And because they are filled with the conceit of wisdom instead of real wisdom they will be a burden to society.[19]

Cultural critic Neil Postman points out that Socrates' story teaches an important lesson for the twenty-first century. King Thamus, who is opposed to writing, and Theuth, who heralds the promise of writing, are both "one-eyed prophets." Each sees with the opposite eye closed; each speaks a measure of truth while simultaneously conveying a subtle error. People and cultures benefit from both a right-brain, intuitive, storycentric approach AND a left-brain, rational, literacy-based approach.[20]

According to the Gospel of Luke two men were walking on the road to Emmaus on the day Jesus had been raised from the dead. These two definitely possessed the head knowledge concerning Jesus of Nazareth, including accurate information about His reputation, His trial, and His resurrection. Yet this information alone made little difference in their lives. They were downcast and discouraged. Luke records, "And he (Jesus) said to them, 'O foolish ones, and slow of heart to believe . . .'" (Luke 24:25). He then opened to them the message of the Scriptures. Somehow, they experienced His presence along the way. Their eyes were opened, and they were changed. Their hearts "burned" with renewed hope, and they acted on their recharged faith. Jesus reconnected their heads with their hearts.

We can know the truth of God's Word with precision and objectivity. Yet the Bible is not merely—or even primarily—a collection of objective propositions. It is a Grand Story—declaring who God is and what He has done as told through dozens of different authorial perspectives, diverse social settings, and stories. The message is multilayered, textured, and expansive. With intellectual precision we can examine the Word and fill our minds with the knowledge of the truth. And with passion in our hearts we can be filled with God-given emotion and desire. We need both eyes to see clearly.

We should never discourage literacy. God's Word has come to us through a written text. Believers and leaders that start with story will need the whole counsel of God. In fact, a storycentric approach should promote and propel literacy and Bible translation in communities. Literacy is important. But let's not blindly require storycentric learners to read as a prerequisite for spiritual maturity. And let's not create the unnecessary hoop of literacy for Christ-centered leaders in storycentric communities. We must be cautious that our zealousness for literacy does not distort our thinking, our influence, and the teaching and influence of others.

It is not a matter of "either-or," but rather of "both-and." The Bible gives the model. There are examples throughout the Scriptures where the written word of God and the spoken word of God are given prominence, often side by side. God determined that Moses should write down the words of the Law (Deut 31–33). He also instructed him to write down the words in a song. Then He instructed Moses to teach the song to the Israelites so that they would have it in their hearts and on their lips continually and remember it always.

STORY ENHANCES LITERACY

While in graduate school, Chuck realized that he wanted to develop as a better writer. Searching for answers outside of himself, he connected with a teacher who was particularly gifted in English literature and classical studies. Chuck asked the teacher how someone can become a better writer.. The teacher recommended that he read *out loud* good stories like C. S. Lewis's *The Chronicles of Narnia*. Chuck learned that listening to good stories, even if it is just hearing yourself, can promote writing and language skills.

Literacy is enhanced by using and teaching story. Story structure allows learners to better visualize context. It encourages people to better anticipate and apply understanding, meaning, and relevance. And it enables people to better communicate in real-world situations through reading, writing, speaking, listening, and thought processing. Story structure actually influences and accelerates literacy.

After looking at the benefits of literacy and the "dark side" of literacy, there are several things that we can conclude in relation to story. First, fact and feeling should not be pitted against each other. Story and literacy should not be at odds. Properly used, story can actually enhance literacy so that the whole counsel of God can be presented, embraced, and lived. Second, story can provide the foundation for logical thinking and argument, writing and exposition, and informative and persuasive structures. Third, research demonstrates that if you want to promote literacy, you should start with story.

Story Develops Thinking

Story matches the way human minds naturally think and process information. It fact, story structure can improve all modes of human thinking. The National Council of Teachers of English states,

> Story is the best vehicle for passing on factual information. Historical figures and events linger in minds when communicated by way of narrative. The ways of other cultures, both ancient and living, acquire honor in story. The facts about how plants and animals develop, how numbers work, or how government policy influence history—any topic for that matter—can be incorporated into story form and made more memorable.[21]

We humans live, think, and learn through stories. Research clearly shows that teaching factual, conceptual, and tacit information is more effectively and efficiently achieved through material formed into story structure. Placing key concepts and information within the structure of stories can provide increased motivation to absorb and learn new and unfamiliar material. Through stories and the context and relevance provided, logical thinking can be developed. Research underscores that a storycentric approach can increase both learning and interest in the topic at hand.

Story Increases Comprehension

Without exception, research studies praise the ability of storycentric instruction to improve comprehension. Stories, rather than logical arguments, are more effective in helping people process and derive meaning, especially when the topic of information is unfamiliar.

Researchers who have studied reading and listening comprehension universally support the idea that people more readily comprehend and retain key narrative information and concepts when they are presented in story form.[22] Stories bring evidence to life. It may be the *information* you want to communicate, but it's the *story* that creates context and relevance so that it is memorable. It may be an *objective* or *goal* you want to get across, but it is the *story*, the obstacles and struggles, that make it comprehensible. It may be the *concepts* you want to present, but the *story characters* and their intentions give readers a reason to care about those concepts.

Hopefully this introduction to story and literacy has gotten you "tilting your head" as you contemplate these ideas. Story and literacy should not be at odds. They can complement one another. A proper understanding and practice of story actually encourages and enhances literacy. Story is a viable way of learning, and in most places of the world, it is the *preferred* way of learning. But story is even more than that. As we'll see in the next chapter, story is a guide to life.

CHAPTER 2 SUMMARY

- Literacy benefits individuals and societies by providing quality of life, economic opportunity, political voice and social security, and legal rights.
- Literacy is a liberating activity and enhances the socio-economic status of many communities.
- Literacy and the Western Enlightenment also have a "dark side" due to an excessive emphasis on rationalism.
- "Left brain" preference has restructured people's worldview, made efficiency king, created suspicion toward feelings, and caused capable leaders to be overlooked.
- Research indicates that story actually enhances one's capacity for literacy, improves all modes of human thinking, and increases comprehension.

3
STORY AS A GUIDE TO LIFE

Why are we entranced by a good story? What's the appeal? What causes us to yawn during a speaker's lecture, yet wake up as soon as she starts to tell a story? Reviews from over 350 research studies representing fifteen separate fields of discipline conclude that story is an effective vehicle for teaching, for motivating, and for the general communication of facts, concepts, and tacit information. Each and every one of these independent sources agrees that story serves effectively to inspire, inform, and educate. There is not one shred of evidence to the contrary.[1] Story is enlivening as well as enlightening, energizing, and informative. Humans rely on story as the primary roadmap for remembering and making sense of life.

Let's review what we mean by story. Our use of the term *story* refers to the "scaffolding" that aids in communication, retention, and application. Regardless of the story's content, story provides a framework for characters that experience conflict and face challenges in their quest to reach a goal or resolution. Story contains characters with which the listener can identify. Story describes the character's motives and obstacles along the way. In an effective story, events happen not for their own sake, but to personify a familiar human dilemma. In this context, story is effective because it naturally triggers the mind to extract meaning and attach relevance to important life principles. In short, story holds up a mirror for the hearer's reflection.

Every culture has passed down true stories as well as myths, fables, legends, and folktales that contribute toward the survival of their societies. People have been telling stories since the dawn of time. On the other hand, written communication is far more recent. Literacy is thought to have begun with the Sumerians and the Egyptians. However, most Western people began to read and write only a few hundred years ago. Before that, story was the leading form through which history, news, values, cultural heritage, and attitudes were passed from person to person and from generation to generation. Today, most of the world's people, even those who can read and write, still pass on information in storycentric forms. We are all hardwired to think, to perceive, and to respond through story.

Numerous studies indicate that humans really do think in story terms. For example, developmental psychologist Roger Schank stated that stories form the framework in which humans sort, understand, and relate experience into memory.[2] Eminent psychologist Jerome Bruner believes that the structure of story is so powerful that our minds automatically use story elements, relationships, and architecture to make sense of the real-world events and the people around us.[3] Mark Turner, Professor at Case Western Reserve University and director of the Cognitive Science Network, concluded that most of our experience, knowledge, and thinking are organized as stories.[4] Story consultant Kendall Haven adds, "It would seem that stories and their supporting evidence are universal. It is an intrinsically human thing to do. We rely on stories like we rely on air, water, sleep, and food. Proving the value of story should feel like an exercise in proving the obvious—something everyone already knows."[5] The expert voices agree that story is a fundamental building block for interpreting the world around us.

We are not saying that developing a story structure is easy. Flannery O'Connor is known to have said, "I find that most people know what a story is until they sit down to write one." Storytelling is a craft. Molding principles into a story framework requires a pinch of inspiration and a bunch of perspiration. This narrative advantage comes at a price. Shaping a story takes repeated trial and error, and trying to write a good story can be humbling and difficult.

But it is worth the price.

People understand events and actions best when viewed from the perspective of a character in a story. Research and real life tell us that stories are highly effective to motivate, to teach, and to communicate attitudes, beliefs, and values. Stories can serve as a foundation in communication and education, and as we will see, they can serve as an effective tool in Christ-centered leadership development.

Looking from this story perspective, then, how do we communicate the timeless truths of Scripture effectively?

STORY IN BIBLICAL TIMES

The Bible begins not with an explanation, but with a story. The story of reconciliation starts at the beginning and goes to the end. It is essentially chronological. The story starts in Genesis when God is alone in the universe. Then He creates. There are characters, conflicts, challenges, and accomplishments. There are successes, failures, interactions, and interventions. There are principles, truths, practical experiences, and moral lessons. The biblical story comes full circle finishing in Revelation with God's re-creation and the total fulfillment of His purposes.

The Bible, as the Grand Narrative, does not rush through the reconciliation story. There is no hurrying through the Old Testament to get to the incarnation of Jesus. As we traverse the stories, we read the unfolding drama of redemption as we walk with real people, struggling through real events, moving towards a real goal.

Yet this is not the usual way literacy-based learners communicate the Scriptures. We often teach as we have been taught. The typical mode is to construct a series of abstract, propositional statements through hours of personal study. We offer a formulaic approach that solves the human dilemma in short order. We become frustrated when those within earshot don't seem to be listening. And we scratch our heads when our listeners can't remember and apply what we have so *clearly* communicated.

Can we do better? Yes, we can. A good place to start is to ask, How does the Bible itself communicate? More specifically, how did Jesus and the Apostle Paul teach?

Jesus and Story

No one communicated as well as Jesus. His words were clear and compelling. He is a supreme model of how to teach. Jesus knew the power of story, and His primary teaching method was story-telling—so much so that the word *parable* has come to be associated with His teaching. For Jesus, *not* using story was the exception. As the Master Teacher, He was sensitive and thoughtful towards His audience. According to John 1:14, Jesus became human to demonstrate God's willingness to meet humanity on our terms. He spoke the language of the people so that they could understand and confront eternal realities.

In the predominately nonliterate society of His day, Jesus used storytelling liberally to ignite the imaginations and emotions of His listeners. His storytelling also drew sharp response from others—some positive, others negative. And His storytelling provoked powerful reactions. Some responded by following Him, and others by rejecting Him. But few remained neutral. That's the power of story.

The stories of Jesus' life and teachings circulated in a storycentric form years before the Gospels were written. Eyewitnesses merely told what they had seen and heard. God entrusted the truth of His Son and salvation to story. During this time period, Christianity grew dramatically, spreading from Judea and Galilee around the Mediterranean Sea and into the interiors of Asia, Africa, and Europe. Although the Jewish leaders viewed Jesus' followers as "uneducated and untrained," these followers of the Way were incredibly effective witnesses. Transformed by God's Spirit, they went everywhere telling the stories they heard and the experiences they had with God. Storycentric people became mature believers, leading the church and changing the world. Even when the Scriptures were available, they continued to communicate the truth in the manner they were taught. They taught the Scriptures through story.

Even Jesus' teaching on prayer employed story. Jesus modeled prayer until the disciples asked Him to teach them to pray (Luke 11; Matt 6). In response, He taught them a prayer in outline form and offered them teaching points—such as don't pray in public for the praise of others like the Pharisees and don't heap up empty phrases like the Gentiles—but nearly all the rest of His teaching on prayer is in a storycentric form. He told the story of the son asking his father for bread in order to teach how our Father in heaven gives good gifts to those who ask. He told the parable of the persistent widow (Luke 18:1–8) to show them that "they ought always pray and not lose heart." He told the parable of the Pharisee and tax collector (Luke 18:9–14) to show the kind of humble attitude God accepts.

Jesus used story in situations where we might be tempted to jump straight to abstract teaching. For example, Peter asked Jesus, "How often will my brother sin against me, and I forgive him? As many as seven times?" Jesus answered with a direct one-liner: "I do not say to you seven times, but seventy-seven times." Then He related the story of the unmerciful servant and concluded with, "So also my heavenly Father will do to every one of you, if you do not forgive your brother from your heart" (Matt 18:22–35).

Suppose you are listening to a speaker teach about God's desire to have a relationship with sinful human beings. The sermon outline might be: (1) God is perfect; (2) People have sinned; (3) Jesus, God's Son, paid the debt for sin; and (4) We can be restored to God through Jesus. All of these points are absolutely true. But now contrast that sermon outline with the following story:

> There was a man who had two sons. And the younger of them said to his father, "Father, give me the share of the property that is coming to me." . . . Not many days later, the younger son gathered all he had and took a journey into a far country, and

there he squandered his property in reckless living.
... But when he came to himself, he said, ... "I will
arise and go to my father." ... But while he was still
a long way off, his father saw him ... and ran and
embraced him and kissed him (Luke 15:11–32).

Through the centuries, this second approach has tugged at
people's hearts. The story has staying power and draws us into a
deeper relationship with God.

Paul and Story

Literate-based learners often challenge the notion of story by
emphasizing the letters of Paul in the New Testament. Paul is not
someone with whom we naturally associate with the description
of "storyteller." Yet the examples we have of his sermons certainly
contain story. And if we look closely, we find that Paul's letters come
out of his experiences. They come out of his own life story.

On his first missionary journey, Paul taught at the synagogue
in Pisidian Antioch by using a story. This story, found in Acts 13,
started with the Exodus, moved through the conquest of Canaan
and the Promised Land, and made its way through the reigns of
Saul and David before finally coming to Jesus, the Christ. Both here
and in his earlier sermons, the apostle masterfully wove the stories
and prophecies of the Old Testament into the story of Jesus—
probably in much the same way that Jesus Himself did on the road
to Emmaus (Luke 24). Twice Paul used his own testimony when he
spoke (Acts 22; 26), weaving in what he had learned about Jesus and
the prophecies of the Old Testament.

Our modern preaching has often taken Paul as a model, but
perhaps we have really taken only his written letters as our model
rather than what we know of his spoken teaching. Like most of us,
Paul's verbal communication differed from his written letters.

What would happen if we used a storycentric approach by
commenting on and applying Scripture's stories to our lives? What

would happen if we used the teaching in Paul's letters as backup to the biblical stories rather than the reverse? Would our listeners engage more actively with the timeless truths embedded within?

Many sermons we hear are abstract, like the ones I heard during my Bible college and seminary years and the ones I taught early in my ministry. It's our culture, it's "how we do things around here." Perhaps we need to examine our method of communication, the audience we want to reach, and the impact we are having on the listeners.

I am not saying that all of Scripture needs to be woven into narrative form. The Bible does contain non-narrative teaching. The whole counsel of God is of vital importance, yet the biblical authors under the Spirit's inspiration started with and majored on story. What does this suggest in terms of where we should start communicating the Word of God?

STORY IN TODAY'S WORLD

Story has a pivotal role today as it did in New Testament times. In our age, when Keynote and PowerPoint have enabled fancier graphics and flashier presentations, storycentric teaching and learning is still a very effective way to communicate. Literate learners and storycentric learners are not all that different when it comes to story. The storycentric communication approach was highly impactful when Jesus walked the earth, and it is still transformational around the world in this high-tech century. From Nike to NASA, major corporations are using story as a key leadership tool. We are coming to realize once again that a great story engages our minds, alters our worldview, touches our lives, and leads to action.

Story Engages Our Minds

We all enjoy a good story, whether it's a well-written novel, a movie with a riveting plot, or a friend narrating something that happened last week. The reason we feel so in tune is a physiological one: story activates our brain in new ways. When we listen to a lecture with bullet points, for example, only the language-processing part of our brain is engaged. However, when we are told a story, additional areas of the brain kick into gear, in order to experience the events of the story. Jerome Bruner's research discovered that story forces our brains to compare data already stored in the brain to the new experiences introduced within the story.[6] This happens in order to interpret new information and create meaning from it. Kathy Maxwell's research suggests that story evokes not only an emotional response that can be measured anecdotally but also a *biological* response that can be measured scientifically. Story physically affects the brain in ways that encourage audience participation, which results in more effective retention, engagement, and character formation.[7] It is a biological fact that we are hardwired to engage with story.

Sometimes story is the *only* way people are willing to listen. Story can present difficult or complex subjects in such a framework that it increases the hearer's capacity to learn. Story gives new ideas more chance to gain traction, and it provides a better opportunity for attitudes to soften.

Bill was a high school history teacher in the Seattle area for his thirty-year career. Many will compare high school history classes to Chinese water torture, but Bill's students experienced something entirely different. He instilled in them a love for history by teaching all his classes through story—often in character dress. For example, he would dramatize how General Sherman went through Georgia "like a hot knife through butter."[8] He would provide details of what was happening in the mind of the soldiers, share the letters of their loved ones, and describe both the successes and the foibles. His students felt like they, too, were marching with the soldiers. Bill provided the stuff that was not in the history books. His students would often do additional research to add to the captivating classroom adventures. It is no surprise that students flocked to his classes, and many would remember the fascinating details of American history for the rest of their lives.

Story Alters Our Worldview

In much the same way, God's Word has transforming potential in people's lives when we present it in a story framework, which makes it easier for them to engage with Truth. Many "unresponsive" people groups are not so unresponsive when they hear the Good News in narrative forms. The use of story often helps the biblical message seem less foreign. To illustrate, postmodern thinking embraces the idea that all religions are the same and that truth is relative. This audience often reacts negatively to logical, abstract presentations, tending to distrust "truth" that is expressed propositionally as dogmatic and confrontational. Upon hearing a lecture, postmoderns generally think, "What are you trying to force upon me?" and they mentally switch off (if not physically walk out). Telling them a story will often avoid this difficulty, for when Truth is embedded in story, people tend to recover their own stories in the light of God's Story.

A storycentric approach not only reduces resistance, but it can over time actually alter the hearer's worldview. According to Merriam-Webster's dictionary, "worldview is the way someone thinks about the world." It is a collection of assumptions individuals hold about the world they live in and their place in it. More specifically, our worldview can be defined as *a set of subconscious mental images that guides what we believe to be real, what we perceive to be important, and how we behave toward others.*

Communication theory also teaches that all of our most firmly held convictions are in the form of mental images. The images that reside in our minds are developed and remembered based on past experiences. I have often tested this premise with an experiment. In conversation with others, I will ask, "What comes to your mind when I say the word 'wedding'?" The responses I get are quite varied, but they often include "bride," "white dress," "vows," "rings," "flowers," and "dancing." Some recount portions of their own wedding or relate a story about another bride or groom they knew. Still others have told about something bizarre or unusual that happened during a wedding they attended. But no one has ever responded to my question with a theological answer such as, "A wedding is the spiritual union of two individuals into one in the sight of God." Our beliefs and values are embedded in our minds not as abstract concepts, but as images and stories that are born out of our experiences.

Even in our enlightened, rational age, story remains at the foundation of our lives. In a culture of iPhones and ThinkPads, the words "Once upon a time . . ." and "That reminds me of a story . . ." are still primary pathways to meaning and relevance. Theologian N. T. Wright explains,

> Stories are, actually, particularly good at modifying or subverting other stories and their worldviews. Where a head-on attack would certainly fail, the parable hides the wisdom of the serpent behind the innocence of the dove, gaining entrance and favor which can then be used to change assumptions which the hearer would otherwise keep hidden for safety.[9]

With our rational, literacy-based approaches, we often lack patience and want to see rapid results, which often leads to only surface change. A storycentric approach, on the other hand, takes the time needed for God to change people from the inside out.

Story Touches Our Lives

One reason we like listening to stories is because we can relate and respond to the characters and situations. The retailer Land's End has for years had this corporate philosophy: "Guaranteed. Period." It is their registered trademark. Initially, the challenge was to get employees to understand and adopt the attitude behind the motto. The company used traditional lecture methods in training programs, but these failed to produce noticeable results. Finally, they settled on a training approach that employed the liberal use of personal stories. Land's End trainers shared stories about employees who had taken the initiative to do whatever was within reason to make their customers happy. Eventually motivation and enthusiasm levels among the staff improved markedly. Soon the sales force had a number of their own stories to tell at seminars, and employees were competing to show good service. Land's End has compiled booklets containing stories that demonstrate how each employee goes the distance for customers. Story has enhanced a sense of belonging, camaraderie, and team building in this company.

Ministry leaders can take a cue from the corporate world in making use of story to touch people's lives. The gospel is being proclaimed and leadership training is being provided to more people now than at any other time in history, yet many of these people are not really *hearing* it. What is unfortunate is that many ministry leaders do not realize the magnitude of the problem. Those affected by a predominately literacy-based approach include the 5.7 billion who live in storycentric communities. Many of these highly intelligent people, both literate and nonliterate, prefer to take in new information apart from abstract, propositional, linear means. Storycentric communities are found in every cultural group in the world, and they are particularly prevalent in the most unreached, most unengaged places on the globe. Through story, the desire and motivation for literacy can be enhanced, and story can increase in anyone—literate or not—a hunger to digest the Good News. What could be a more worthy goal!

If our most deeply held convictions are in the form of images, then the only sure way to touch people's lives is to replace their current images with more powerful ones. Sadly, most Christian leaders have been attempting—with largely unsuccessful results— to change people's convictions by replacing images with concepts. Many Western ministry leaders with whom I am acquainted have been trained theologically in formal academic settings, so they are more comfortable with the transmission of truth via carefully reasoned, abstract theological constructs to their listeners. But it doesn't seem to be working to change the listeners' lives.

Ministry leaders from several African nations recently told me that story plays a vital role in both shaping and preserving their cultures. Like all communities, most of their shared core beliefs are passed from generation to generation through true stories, legends, and songs. These narratives embody the essence of what they consider important for their children and grandchildren to know. Even as they welcome the kind of education that brings socio-economic advancement, these leaders are concerned that their communities will make the mistake of teaching the next generations with a literacy-based, conceptual approach that disconnects them from their own story.

Let me illustrate. Story has contributed dramatically to our culture's evolving views of acceptable sexual behavior within the span of a generation. Our collective perception of sexual relations outside the bonds of traditional marriage has morphed from predominantly negative to overwhelmingly positive. Hollywood's producers, directors, and scriptwriters have indisputably wielded a formidable hand in this seismic shift through effective storytelling.

While Hollywood is winning over the culture by telling better stories, Christian efforts to shape minds and hearts with reason and logic alone is akin to holding back the ocean's tide with a plastic bucket and toy shovel. It is not enough that our reason and logic be correct and true. The succeeding generations need more than doctrine and abstract theology strung together with biblical proof texts to shape their beliefs and preserve the values we hold so dearly. Our children need to know how the biblical story relates to their own stories. They need to know the church's 2,000-year-old story that dramatically affects their lives today. These images embedded by story form our deepest convictions, and more powerful images informed by alternate experiences touches people's lives.

Josh teaches an adult class at his church. Because the church is located close to a seminary, a number of graduate students and teachers attend his class. One morning he started the class with this comment: "We are going to do things differently today. I encourage you to close your Bibles and just listen." This stirred things up a bit as several members made sure they had their "sword" even more firmly in their grasp. Josh opened to a modern-day translation of 2 Samuel 6, which tells the story about the Ark of the Covenant being returned to Jerusalem and David dancing before the Lord. All Josh did was read the text dramatically; he did not add or delete a single word from the recorded text. Occasionally he would pause to ask questions related to the reading. At first the class was hesitant to respond, but over the course of the hour they warmed up to the idea and became engaged. After each Q&A session, Josh would return to the story and read the next bit. Questions followed the difficult passage about Uzzah and the Ark, and the David and Michal section likewise elicited another set of questions. The class time was filled with nothing more than reading the story and asking questions.

Josh had done substantial preparatory study and knew where he wanted the discussion to lead, but he allowed the class—including the seminary students and professors present—to "discover" the truth on their own. When the class was over, participants approached Josh and said, "That was amazing! I have read that text many times, but today it came to life! I will never forget this." This is the power of story to touch lives.

Story Leads to Action

Whether people are literacy-based or storycentric, story makes a dramatic impact on the listeners. For example, a friend in South Asia is an author and ministry leader. He is highly literate and has an earned a PhD, but he comes alive when biblical truth is communicated through story. It touches his heart, influences his mind, and challenges him to live all the more for Jesus Christ. In the end, story leads to greater response and action on the part of the hearer.

In *A Treatise of Human Nature* (1739), philosopher David Hume concluded that desire rather than reason determines human behavior. He believed that it is vain to expect that any logic, divorced from the affections, will ever engage people to embrace sounder principles. Story is critical because moral decisions and behavior are not primarily a cerebral affair in which we dispassionately weigh arguments about rights and justice. Rather, most moral action resides in people's intuitions and emotional processes. And, as we saw in Jay Winsten's Designated Driver campaign, reasoning matters most when story catalyzes reason to consider new responses.

Jesus employed the power of story to challenge people's thinking and behavior (Mark 4:33). Whether addressing His disciples, the crowds, or the religious leaders, Jesus often created stories rich with familiar images to reveal prejudices, false assumptions, and the need for fundamental change. For His storycentric listeners, this approach was so radical that some sacrificed all to follow Him while others plotted to kill Him. In my own experience, people respond powerfully both to fictional and non-fictional story, and many have made life-altering decisions upon hearing a moving, well-told tale. Moreover, younger leaders I have mentored are indelibly shaped, encouraged, and motivated by the stories of my personal failures and victories.

STORY FOR TODAY'S LEADERS

Today's emerging leaders gravitate toward story not because they are less intelligent but because of their preferred learning preference. Ryan is part of the "millennial" generation in America. He is preparing to pastor a church. He recently graduated from a reputable college with highest honors—summa cum laude. Yet when he heard a description of storycentric learning, he exclaimed, "That's me! In my heart, I'm a storycentric learner."

This phenomenon is increasingly evident within our literate culture as well as nonliterate populations. A study of lay pastors in South Asia found that those who were trained by storycentric methods communicated biblical truth more accurately than their literate counterparts who were trained with print-based curriculum. Furthermore, the literacy-based group displayed a greater tendency to teach syncretized (heretical) doctrinal positions.

Similar results surfaced using a storycentric approach to develop leaders in North Africa. Seventeen nonliterate and semi-literate young men underwent a two-year leadership training program using Bible stories told in chronological order. At the end of the period, all men had mastered approximately 135 biblical stories in their correct chronological order, spanning from Genesis to Revelation. They were able to tell the stories, sing songs for each story, and enact dramas about each of the stories. When seminary professors from the US arrived to give them a six-hour oral exam, the students demonstrated the ability to answer questions about both the facts and the theology of the stories. They also showed an excellent grasp of the gospel message, the nature of God, and their new life in Christ, quickly and skillfully referring to the stories to answer a variety of doctrinal questions. Given a theological theme, they could accurately name multiple biblical stories in which that theme occurs. If asked, they could tell each story and elaborate on how it addressed the theme. Their understanding was found to be far superior to colleagues who attended a resident literacy-based Bible college. The testing professors concluded:

> The training process has successfully achieved its goals of enabling students to tell a large number of biblical stories accurately, to have a good under-standing of those stories and the theology that they convey and to have an eagerness to share the Christian message. The community received the stories and story-songs enthusiastically and made them a part of the church and church life alike.[10]

The church has been led by scholars for so long that we have distorted ideas about Christian discipleship and especially Christian leadership. Some of us doubt whether nonliterate pastors can possibly lead others into spiritual maturity. The conventional adage goes, "If you don't read, you can't lead."

Yet it is worth remembering that among the first disciples were fishermen, tax collectors, a doctor, and at least one Zealot. We don't know the occupation of the others, but Jesus certainly did not entrust the Great Commission exclusively to scholars. And we do know that those storycentric leaders took the gospel and created Christ-centered communities that met in homes, shared life together, and were active in their faith.

In today's literacy-based church, if you want to grow in Christ, you typically study more. Christian growth has been inevitably tied to an academic path. We just keep going to school. I have great respect for the rigorous pursuit of truth, but Jesus also called for action. When He selected His first students, He taught them truth for three years—by doing, in action, and with people. When they graduated, He sent them out into the world saying, "You don't know everything, but you know enough. You'll have a Guide, and I'll be with you always. So go and teach the world to obey my commands" (Matt 28:20, my paraphrase). *And they went and did it.*

In the following section, I'll talk about the challenge of developing Christ-centered, storycentric leaders. These leaders are specially chosen by God to be a blessing to their communities, and they can make an important contribution to the global church through the power of story that is at the heart of their cultures.

CHAPTER 3 SUMMARY

- Every culture has passed down stories that teach essential values and contribute toward the survival of their societies.
- The Bible is the Grand Narrative. The Scriptures are not primarily an explanation; rather, they begin, continue, and end with story.
- Jesus often used story to communicate to his listeners, and Paul the Apostle often employed story in his verbal communication.
- Today story engages our minds, alters our worldview, touches our lives, and leads to action.

PART TWO

Leadership Development

4
IN SEARCH OF LEADERSHIP

A Google search of "leadership development" currently yields more than 121,000,000 results. Both for-profit and not-for-profit organizations invest billions of dollars each year on strategies intended to develop leaders. The pervasive shortage of talented leaders in all spheres of private and public life teases our appetite for solutions.

Leadership makes a difference in every sector of life—for good or for ill. Churches and ministries around the world are convinced that effective leadership makes a positive difference. They also have turned en masse in search of ways to cultivate individuals who can provide effective leadership. These frenetic attempts to develop leaders show no signs of slowing down, and will likely continue to expand markedly into storycentric communities in the decades ahead.

Although societies have advocated the critical role of leaders for thousands of years, structured programs that attempt to develop leaders in the private sector are a relatively recent phenomenon. Various military branches have a longer track record in the leadership discipline, but most entities only began to launch leadership initiatives since World War II. What accounts for the dramatic upsurge of interest and activity around leadership development? What factors contribute toward the explosive emphasis on leadership in our time? A look at some historical motivators that provided the impetus for the phenomenon of leadership development today will help us to better understand the current situation.

HISTORICAL MOTIVATORS

The increase of leadership development efforts can be traced to at least three intersecting factors that converged in the evolution of modern organizational life: (1) evolving leadership studies, 2) shifting organizational needs, and (3) a lack of available leaders.

Evolving Leadership Studies

The first contributing factor that caused the increase of leadership development efforts was evolving research in leadership studies. Researchers in the nineteenth century examined the talent and skills of successful leaders who had risen to power. Their study of men like Julius Caesar, Napoleon, and Abraham Lincoln led to the development of "trait theory" or "great man theory." (Given the male-centrism of the day, women were not included in these studies.) In these and other cases it seemed that the right man had appeared at the right time to take hold of a situation to lead a group of people into safety or success.

A leading researcher, Thomas Carlyle, proposed a number of characteristics that distinguished leaders from non-leaders—traits such as dominance, persistence, socioeconomic status, and self-confidence.[1] The leaders studied were often aristocratic rulers who achieved their position through birthright. Since people of lesser social status had fewer opportunities to practice and achieve leadership roles, it fueled the idea that the most important leadership traits are inherited. In other words, leaders are born, not developed. This trait-based perspective dominated most empirical and theoretical work in leadership until the mid-twentieth century. Most studies did not consider the development of leaders as necessary or even plausible.

But all that changed shortly after World War II. Researchers such as Ralph Stogdill[2] and R. D. Mann[3] began to uncover a drastically different reality of the driving forces behind leadership. Their studies found that individuals who are effective leaders in one situation may not necessarily be effective leaders in other situations. The evolving leadership studies in the mid-twentieth century began to view leadership not as an inherited set of traits, but as "contingent" upon a person's leadership style in relation to the surrounding environment. This view suggests that people can be effective leaders under certain circumstances, but not under others. This paradigm shift shaped the future of leadership studies throughout the subsequent decades. The White Stag Leadership Development program, which began in 1958, was one of the first modern initiatives. The first formalized programs to develop leaders specifically for Christian ministries followed over a decade later.

This new leadership research was a primary contributing factor in the advent of leadership development initiatives since it suggested, for the first time, that developing leaders is not only possible but is actually necessary to help individuals reach their leadership potential. Jim Kouzes and Barry Posner reflect the modern mood when they say in *The Leadership Challenge*, "Contrary to the myth that only a lucky few can ever decipher the mystery of leadership, our research has shown us that leadership is an observable, learnable set of practices."[4]

The perspective towards leaders thus evolved from the nineteenth century view that leaders are born and not developed to the mid-twentieth century view that leaders can, in fact, be developed. This research caused an upsurge in focus on bringing up a new generation of leaders.

Shifting Organizational Needs

The second factor that contributed to the increase of leadership development efforts was shifting organizational needs. Prior to World War II, plants and factories that had come of age during the Industrial Revolution needed managers. But when the tanks stopped rolling in 1945, they would increasingly need leaders for changing organizational roles.

Much has been written about the similarities and differences between management and leadership. There is general agreement among scholars that the disciplines overlap, but there are also distinct emphases in each (see chart below). While the management role tends to focus on maintaining and monitoring systems, the leadership role aligns people to work together effectively. Managers are appointed with organizational authority to position-specific roles, while leaders refer to those with or without formal authority. Managers contribute primarily to ensure organizational stability; leaders enable organizational stakeholders to work their way through change, or to face the disintegration of familiar structures and processes.

MANAGEMENT	LEADERSHIP
Planning and budgeting: Detailed steps and timetables for achieving needed results, then allocating resources necessary to make it happen.	*Establishing direction:* Developing a vision of the future and strategies for producing the changes needed to achieve that vision.
Organizing and staffing: Establishing structure for accomplishing plans, staffing that structure with individuals, delegating responsibility and authority for carrying out the plan, providing policies and procedures to help guide people, and creating systems to ensure implementation.	*Aligning people:* Communicating direction in words and deeds to everyone whose cooperation may be needed, so as to influence the creation of teams that understand and accept the vision and strategies.
Controlling and problem solving: Monitoring results, identifying deviation from plan, then organizing to solve these problems.	*Motivating and inspiring:* Energizing people to overcome major political, bureaucratic, and resource barriers to change by satisfying basic, but often unfulfilled, human needs.
Results in predictability: Produces short-term results expected by various stakeholders (customers, stockholders, employees, government regulators).	*Results in change:* Produces useful change (new products, new approaches, new values) often to a dramatic degree.

During the zenith of the Industrial Age, organizations needed managers who were competent primarily to maintain and monitor systems. This emphasis was reflected in university programs and research during the early twentieth century that focused most of their attention on management solutions to attend the organizational assembly lines. Management terms such as "systems theory," "span of control," and "bureaucracy" became popular in organizations.

In 1945, when war in Europe and the Pacific ended, a new era in Western culture was birthed that would have a ripple effect around the globe over the next generation. This new era was characterized by an ever-increasing rate of change. Due to escalating competitiveness, continuous restructuring activities, regular demographic changes in the workforce, stakeholder demands, and rapid technological progress, the critical need in organizations morphed from managers who could maintain and monitor systems to strategic leaders who could challenge, motivate, and mobilize people in a rapidly changing cultural climate. "Challenging the process," "inspiring a shared vision," and "enabling others to act" became the new leadership mantra. Although competent management continued to be necessary, organizational energy and budgets reflected shifting priorities to cultivate competent leaders for the changing world.

Lack of Available Leaders

The third intersecting factor for the recent upsurge in leadership development efforts was the declining pool of available leaders.

This was not the case historically. Throughout recorded civilization, a process traditionally known as "mentoring" was the primary means of passing on knowledge, skills, and leadership in nearly every field and in nearly every culture. This relational approach to developing leaders dates back to Greek mythology. According to Homer, before leaving for the siege of Troy Odysseus entrusted his household, including the welfare of his son Telemachus, to a guardian named Mentor. Hence the term "mentoring." For the next ten years, the older and more experienced Mentor functioned as teacher, adviser, and friend to Telemachus. Mentor was responsible for the total development of Odysseus's son, which encompassed almost every facet of his life. Homer's story reflects one of the oldest attempts by a society to describe how leaders are developed and how important leadership behaviors and values are passed to successive generations.

These principles of mentoring were key elements for the continuity of leaders. Young men were often apprenticed to a person who was considered effective in leadership within their chosen vocation. The boy lived with the master, worked his way up, and finally proved himself a master by producing his own exemplary leadership. Even within the church, up until the 1800s, established pastors would often invite young men to live in their home and have them read from their library in order to develop their skills, cultivate their hearts, and challenge their minds towards effective church leadership. Through this mentoring process, societies ensured an ongoing supply of quality leaders.

However, with the advent of industrial society, all that changed. The master-apprentice relationship was replaced by the employer-employee contract. The employer's focus shifted away from ensuring the perpetuity of quality masters and toward increasing productivity. This was due in large part to the fact that industry embraced Frederick Taylor's principles of Scientific Management (which we will examine in chapter 7), in which production is king, efficiciency is queen, and both are more important than people. What profited the employer no longer benefited the employee. The less experienced workers became cogs in the wheel of assembly lines, shouldering the burden of lower wages and longer hours with little hope of advancement. This radical shift was a significant reason for the rise of unions, with worker pitted against management. Although unions provided more profit-sharing in the plant, they did little to develop a new generation of capable leaders. Paul Stanley and J. Robert Clinton have stated that the resultant relational connection between more experienced and less experienced workers has weakened or is nonexistent.[5]

What does all this mean? For hundreds of years, mentoring was the primary means of passing on knowledge and skills to the next generation. Then along came the Industrial Revolution and it drastically changed the dynamics of relationships, to the point that the process of passing on leadership became fractured. In fact, we started to ignore mentoring altogether. Since the person who was passing on their knowledge to the next generation was now nonexistent, a crisis in the number of capable leaders eventually became evident. We're paying the price for this today.

To clarify, this dilemma was not immediately evident during the first generation of leaders after World War II. Both for-profit and not-for-profit sectors of Western society benefited significantly from the military's development of wartime leaders. But as organizations attempted to identify the crop of leaders to succeed the World War II generation, they were alarmed at the severe shortage of likely candidates. This decline of capable emerging leaders was a major contributing factor to the global scramble to develop leaders in organizations and communities.

Let's put this all together. While leadership studies were undergoing a seismic shift with the claim that leaders can in fact be developed, organizations were attempting to accommodate the changing industrial nature of the workplace. Close on the heels of these movements was an acute awareness of the lack of capable leaders as World War II veterans (known as the "Greatest Generation") moved into retirement. With this awareness came the realization that something needed to change. These intersecting historical motivators have created a keen interest in leadership development, and the signals suggest that the tide of those committed to develop leaders will continue to rise.

CHALLENGES FOR THE CHURCH

Like all organizations, the need for leadership development has also become increasingly evident across faith-based sectors, but we face many challenges.

Take the example of Jeff who enrolled at a Bible college because his heart was set on becoming a youth pastor. Four years and a pile of school loans later, Jeff had acquired considerable biblical knowledge and an admirable grasp of his denomination's doctrinal statements. A local church offered him the job of his dreams two weeks after he walked across the stage to receive his diploma.

Jeff was excited to jump into ministry and work with high school students, and very soon his life was consumed with planning youth programs and deeper life retreats. Yet only a small handful of students showed up for the mid-week programs Jeff had so diligently prepared. The students that did show up were more interested in texting their friends than in hearing Jeff's teachings. So Jeff prayed and worked even harder, trying every gimmick he knew to get their attention. He was operating on the assumption that teaching good theology and planning fun events was the same as leading youth. Jeff's intentions were right, but his reasoning and methods were wrong. The senior pastor and church board, assuming that the Bible college had prepared him sufficiently to know how to do his job, offered him little counsel.

When the youth met Jeff's best efforts with lackluster enthusiasm and outright resistance, he eventually resorted to loud and intense scolding in an attempt to motivate them into participation. That strategy backfired too. Several parents launched a complaint campaign against the youth pastor's abrasiveness. Within eighteen months, Jeff was out of the ministry and running a landscaping business.

Jeff's story has been a familiar one in hundreds of churches. Well-intentioned men and women enter ministry with a diploma and a "call," only to learn that they are in the deep end of the pool with inadequate preparation and little access to effective development. Although most Bible colleges and seminaries advertise their commitment to prepare leaders, their efforts are incomplete. Churches, therefore, perceive that these institutions are either incapable of developing leaders for effective ministry or are irrelevant in today's world. But the church is doing little to alleviate the problem, and the attrition rate of emerging church leaders has reached epidemic proportions.

We are living in one of the most exciting eras in church history. In many parts of the world, churches and Christian ministries are multiplying at break-neck speed. Indigenous mission movements are flowering. Our Lord is continuing to expand His kingdom despite persecution and suffering. More and more people are becoming followers of Jesus Christ. House churches are springing up within storycentric communities in country after country. These throngs of new believers, as well as the churches and service ministries emerging among them, need capable, faithful leaders, but the leadership shortage is acute. For this reason, in many places one pastor has to care for multiple congregations. A more robust supply chain of qualified and faithful leadership is desperately needed to keep up with the rapid expansion of the church.

Leadership Development for Emerging Leaders

At the Lausanne 2010 Cape Town Congress, delegate participation was overwhelming at every session on the topic of leadership development. Churches continually solicit men and women who will faithfully and effectively lead congregations in our twenty-first century culture. Also needed are Christ-centered leaders who can apply their God-given wisdom and skills in the arena of public life, those who will exercise leadership influence in the marketplace.

Two projections over the next decade summarize a global challenge. First, since almost half the world's population is under twenty-five, young people will be entering the marketplace in greater numbers and more quickly than we can prepare them. Second, older people will be retiring in greater numbers and more quickly than we can replace them. Unless standards are raised for young people today that will help them think and act like authentic leaders, they will not be ready for the responsibility thrust on them. We have to connect with them, help them interpret the constant swirl of information, model the inherent value of discipline, and provide challenging opportunities in supportive environments. In short, we have to get serious about developing competent, Christ-centered influencers for today and tomorrow.

Many eager emerging leaders are chomping at the bit to assume their sacred trust, but they are ill prepared. In addition, fundamentalist and militant Islam, Hinduism, and Buddhism will test our understanding of how to prepare these emerging leaders for the daunting task of leadership in this century. Globalization, new technology, urbanization, and the postmodern influences of the West will challenge our conventional methods of leadership. Senior leaders are retiring and existing leaders are aging, so the time is now. We must move with thoughtful haste to cultivate leaders for stable succession, just as Jesus cultivated leaders in preparation for His departure.

The story about Jeff is not unique. Denominations report that over 70 percent of their pastors are leaving ministry within their first five years. In the US alone, 1,500 pastors quit every month due to conflict, burnout, or moral failure. A study by *Christianity Today* found that 34 percent of all congregations have forced a pastor to resign due to leadership problems. The same study showed that 41 percent of the churches that forced out their pastors have done this to at least two previous pastors. Various reasons are cited for this trend, but the most glaring problem is a lack of healthy development of leaders.[6]

Several key factors are negatively impacting the church's effectiveness in developing emerging leaders. These factors include a lack of role models, the need for time and patience, competing organizational priorities, and a disregard for leadership succession.

Lack of Role Models

One of the challenges to the church's effectiveness in developing young leaders is a lack of role models. There are just not enough mature, honest, and humble leaders to show the way. Younger men and women with significant leadership potential have left the church because of leaders who lack sufficient experience or know-how about the task of ministry leadership, or who do not lead with integrity.

Many older Christian leaders believe they have learned leadership by trial and error. They refer to themselves as graduates of "the school of hard knocks." Although they may have picked up a few tips from books or teachers along the way, many feel that they themselves have never been on the receiving end of effective leadership development. Therefore, they have neither a practical working knowledge of how leaders are developed nor a clear path to follow. What is more regrettable is that they usually lack a keen interest to develop others.

Bob is president of a Christian ministry. He worked his way up the ranks for thirty years before he was appointed to his leadership role. He is widely respected by his peers, and is regarded as successful by most people in his network. Bob sets a high standard for excellence, and the staff he hires works hard to meet his expectations. But the work environment is brutal, and the average staff tenure is just three years. Bob clearly demonstrates the leadership skills that many emerging leaders around him want to emulate. He has a genuine desire to help them, and has publicly expressed his commitment to develop young leaders, but something is missing. Looking back on his journey, Bob cannot recall any discernible patterns in his own development. "No one developed me," he says, "so how am I supposed to know how to develop others?"

Although Bob has heard much discussion about the need to develop leaders, he is like many who believe that they have learned how to be a good leader mostly through hands-on experience. For them, the idea of developing other leaders intentionally is like learning a foreign language.

In many situations, churches have "grown" but society has not been impacted. As David Bennett observes, "Christian leaders have not demonstrated how to be salt and light. Success is measured in terms of attendance and offerings, rather than the active expression of kingdom of God values."[7] Often the predominant models of leadership for emerging leaders are drawn from the corporate world or from authoritarian cultural patterns, neither of which works over the long haul in the church context.

Time and Patience Needed

A second challenge is the need for time and patience. Leadership development is a process. Developing leaders demands a major commitment over a protracted period of time. Yet in the hustle-bustle modern world, efficiency and effectiveness often take existing leaders away from building into the lives of others. Far too many leaders lack the time to develop or mentor others, which becomes a tangential program or an activity to be delegated rather than a pattern of life for every leader in ministry. Remarked Maia, a thoughtful leader from Ukraine, "We are analyzing the reasons for slow growth of the numbers of leaders. We see that we need to invest ourselves into those capable individuals. So the problem is also in us and how busy we are with other aspects of ministry."[8] Regional and national leaders are in such high demand that leadership development is crowded out; thus the most visible leaders may have the least to contribute from their own example and practice.

In addition, behavioral change happens slowly. In our postmodern world, many of the younger generation, who have great potential, have been negatively impacted by their dysfunctional backgrounds. They need time, patience, and a listening ear. Many have been made fatherless through divorce, orphaned through war, or been victimized by self-inflicted behavior. Developing the next generation of leaders requires a long-term resolve, which is difficult when older leaders are thinking only of the short-term costs.

Competing Priorities

A well-known evangelical mission publicizes leadership excellence as one of its core priorities. This organization has faced dwindling financial contributions for the past several years. During their budget-planning exercises over this period of time, line items associated with leadership development have been greatly reduced or eliminated altogether. Often, when push comes to shove, the priority for developing leaders is less urgent than other observed mission-critical functions.

Today's ministry organizations consistently face tough financial choices. They often struggle with the dilemma of balancing "non-negotiable" ministry demands such as salaries and mortgage payments with initiatives to develop people. Under these difficult circumstances, the developmental programs are often "put on hold until the next budget cycle." Organizations that delay or eliminate these initiatives may be surviving for today, but they are also mortgaging their futures.

Developing leaders is expensive. Professionals that are highly competent in the field of leadership development are rare and often are in high demand. Some ministries may opt for a non-specialist internal person to oversee leadership development, or they may appoint a friend of a friend to assist with developing leaders, or they may disregard leadership development except for lip service. As a result, the quality of leadership development offered within the ministry context is mediocre at best.

Issues of Leadership Succession

Nineteen years ago "Marcell" was living in Thailand when he started an ministry to rescue young girls and boys caught in human trafficking. For nearly two decades he has travelled the globe with tireless passion. He has built a respected ministry with a combination of hard work and charisma. As the ministry has grown, his staff has come to expect his presence and personal involvement in nearly every new initiative. But Marcell is getting older, and is visibly worn with the grind. He worries about the future of the ministry. But when asked about his plans for leadership succession, he comments, "That's God's job, not mine. Just as God anointed me, so He will raise up another to take my place."

Leaders like Marcell believe that God alone is responsible to develop leaders and that, they think, lets them "off the hook."

They harbor the erroneous notion that leaders are born not made, so they say, "Why should we try to develop them?" Some of them also nurture the "once a leader, always a leader" idea, operating on the premise that you only leave the position when you die. The replacement or training of leaders happens only when there is a crisis, when it is absolutely necessary, or when a vacuum is created.

This idea that God alone is responsible for appointing leaders is more spiritualized than biblical. Jesus spent a lion's share of His time and energy developing the disciples for their future leadership. While it is certainly true that God is working out His sovereign purposes by guiding the appointment of leaders to key ministry roles, leaders also have an important part in the process. Marcell's perspective is actually a Christianized version of the "great man" theory of the early twentieth century, which had suggested that leadership comes from nature, not nurture, and that effective leaders are born, not developed. Although this theory has largely been debunked by more thorough research in recent decades, many Christian leaders continue to champion the idea with carefully chosen biblical references that support their view that God unilaterally appoints leaders.

Marcell and many others use scriptural language from a sincere motivation to faithfully serve in their leadership roles, but it has created the fallacious view that leadership is a holy mantle that only God can bestow. This subconsciously absolves the leader of their responsibility for cultivating others, an endeavor that requires time, effort, and commitment.

Although most will not admit this, many leaders don't prepare anyone to take over leadership because they simply don't want to share the position or give up leadership responsibilities, either because they derive their sense of worth from what they do or because they have become addicted to power. They employ the "anointed by God" motif to promote the not-so-subtle sense of their own indispensability. Recently an African pastor publicly and with great pride declared, "When I die, my church will die." As these leaders listen to their admirers, the combination of personal ego and public perception serve up a recipe that reinforces the sense that the leader is irreplaceable. With no intention of giving away responsibility, they are unwilling to expend energy in raising up anyone who could take over their position. A second line of leadership is not developed for fear that the current leaders may lose their jobs. In truth, those who maintain this posture idolize their positions, and have no intention to sacrifice or serve so that others can be raised up.

Leadership Development for Storycentric Leaders

Many Western Christian leaders agree that there has been considerable progress in evangelizing and discipling storycentric people groups using stories and music. Many acknowledge that the use of story is a powerful thing when used correctly in the right context. But what's the right context for leadership development in storycentric communities and among storycentric learners?

Many storycentric leaders have been overlooked or sidelined because they are nonliterate. But as we have seen, storycentric learners, both literate and nonliterate, learn best and communicate most effectively through stories, symbols, and music.

The ability to read should not be a prerequisite for Christ-centered leadership development. In fact, storycentric communities identify their leaders differently than literacy-based societies. In cultures where education is easily available, young people often decide on their own to attend school, and declare they themselves are ready for leadership on the basis of the knowledge they have acquired. Conversely, storycentric communities typically identify and affirm the leader in their midst quite apart from the individual's formal education. This important distinction makes leadership development in storycentric cultures less about identifying and raising up leaders as it is about cultivating Christ-centered leadership competencies within those who are already leading.

Christ-centered leadership development in storycentric communities is a critical need, as it is in every community. Storycentric learners not only can lead, but they can thrive in Christian leadership positions.

Bekele's Story

Bekele Shanko was born into a rural, nonliterate Ethiopian family. Bekele's father worshiped Satan, was addicted to alcohol, and abused his three wives. At the age of four, Bekele was officially dedicated for a lifetime of Satan worship, destined to follow in his father's footsteps. But God had another plan for him.

Despite the absence of a church or Christian witness in his part of Ethiopia, Bekele was introduced to the message of the gospel through a series of incredible events. He was transformed by the living Christ and is being used miraculously by God to bring healing and hope in his country.

Bekele's community, impressed with his leadership gifts, have affirmed him as a leader among them. He is a man who displays deep humility and dependence upon God. He asks probing questions and has a passion to develop as a leader. But despite his keen intellect and courageous faith, Bekele is a storycentric learner.

Who will develop him?

Bekele's story is one among many that signals a global trend among emerging leaders. God is raising up a generation, often in unconventional ways, to lead His church. These incredible accounts highlight God's faithfulness to provide leaders for His church. At the same time, the collective voice of these leaders is also saying things such as:

- We need help to become Christ-centered leaders who will resist the lure of success and advance the kingdom of God in difficult places and against seemingly impossible odds.
- We need contextualized Christ-centered leadership models that are appropriate to specific cultures. We prefer our own indigenous leadership heroes for the future.
- We need mentors who will personally invest in us through ongoing life-upon-life encounters. Leadership training events are not sufficient alone to bring about the Christ-centered perspectives and leadership maturity we desperately long for.

- We need each other. We are motivated by collaboration, not competition. We want to partner with other like-minded kingdom leaders, sharing resources as good stewards in our service to the church and society.
- We need leadership development now. It is an urgent priority for the church in the twenty-first century.

The church worldwide has a bright hope with younger leaders like Bekele, but they need role models—established leaders who will take personal responsibility to invest time and energy to nurture them into maturity. Emerging leaders also need ministries that will work together to develop them to their highest kingdom potential. As these men and women share their heart's cry for development, now is the time to raise up a generation of leaders to advance the whole gospel to the whole world.

CHAPTER 4 SUMMARY

- The recent increase of leadership development efforts is a response to three converging historical motivators: (1) evolving leadership research which confirms that leaders can be developed, (2) shifting organizational needs from managers to leaders, and (3) the declining pool of available leaders across all sectors of society.
- The need to develop ministry leaders is acute; however, the church faces numerous challenges in the development of next-generation leaders: a lack of good role models, the shortage of patience to invest in emerging leaders, competing demands for the organization's resources, and the absence of commitment among existing leaders to raise up others to replace themselves.
- Developing Christ-centered leaders in storycentric contexts is an urgent priority.

THE SCOPE OF LEADERSHIP DEVELOPMENT

With so many people talking about leadership development, one might think that most leaders know and understand the topic. But this is not the case. Let me explain with a story.

THE APPRENTICE AND THE MASTER

"Is experience a good teacher?" the bright apprentice asked the master. "Can I develop as a leader from experience?"

"Some people say that experience is the best teacher," replied the master. "But some experiences don't teach anything."

The apprentice looked surprised. "So experience is not the best teacher?"

"Well, not exactly," said the master. "It's just that not every experience offers important leadership lessons."

"So how do I learn?" asked the apprentice. "What experiences are helpful? What experiences are unhelpful? And how can I tell the difference?"

The master smiled at the apprentice's eagerness. "The experiences that challenge are the best experiences. The experiences that stretch us, that force us to develop new competencies, are the ones that help us grow."

"OK, I get it," said the apprentice. "When I am really pushed to my limits by an experience, I will learn. Is that it?"

"Not exactly. Even when our limits are tested we don't necessarily learn."

The apprentice looked confused. "So you mean I can have challenging experiences that press me to my limits and still not develop as a leader."

"That's right. We also need the good fortune of receiving feedback and support from others. Feedback and reflection allow us to assess how we are doing, what's working, and how we need to change. And we also need the acceptance and encouragement from others if we expect to grow. We simply cannot do it alone."

"Let me see if I understand," said the apprentice slowly. "If I am serious about learning from challenging experiences, and if I get support and feedback with acceptance and encouragement from key people, then I can develop the important leadership skills I need. Right?"

"As far as it goes, yes. But there is still the question of what develops in leadership development."

"What do you mean?"

"You see, there are some things that are developable and other things that appear to be inherited genetically," the master replied. "For example, certain personality characteristics that are shaped through our childhood appear to be set by the time we are adults. So while some factors provide limits to our development, others provide skills and competencies to be developed."

The apprentice sighed. "It all seems so complicated."

"It is complicated," agreed the master. "Learning and growing are not simple or easy. And it takes time. Years, in fact. A lot of pieces have to fit together. We used to think it was easier, that single training events could make it happen. But we were mistaken. Development is part of a larger picture in a leader's life that happens over time in a process."

"Thanks," said the apprentice. "I think I understand now. My development as a leader is a big task that takes a long time."

"Now you're getting the point," said the master with a smile. "And I think you're well on your way."[1]

Leadership Development is Complex

The questions posed by the apprentice are questions that many have asked. In the 1980s, I began to work with emerging leaders with a desire to help them to not just survive but to thrive in ministries. I have tried to understand and teach how leaders learn, grow, and change throughout their lifetimes. Although there is still a lot to learn, what follows are some of my findings based on observation, experience, and research.

Current leadership development efforts seem to resemble the American trailblazers of the Wild West. Modern America began with English colonial settlements in the early seventeenth century, followed by enormous energy focused on westward expansion. It was "wild" because it was a story of conquest, survival, and persistence, a culture of rugged individualism, unregulated behavior, and fierce competition as pioneers staked their claims. Hopes were high, standards were low, with boomtowns turning to ghost towns overnight.

Today, a plethora of initiatives called "leadership development" are popping up in business, education, and among Christian ministries. Leadership development is used to describe everything from seminars for CEOs to boot camps for college students and mentoring programs for pre-schoolers. The concept of leadership development is so overused that the idea has come to mean almost anything related to improving the human condition. The majority of those who launch these initiatives are usually well-intentioned, with their programs aimed at improving the quality of its leaders. Yet the vast majority of leadership development programs are unregulated, lack informed guidance, and have a short shelf life. The budding discipline of leadership development currently resembles the Wild West: it needs credible definitions and processes in order to come to full bloom.

LEADERSHIP EMERGENCE AND LEADERSHIP DEVELOPMENT COMPARED

In order to better understand leadership development, it is essential to differentiate between leadership development and the broader term, leadership emergence. Three major components contribute to a leader's emergence.

The first component that contributes to a leader's emergence is *inherited traits*. Some people inherit more leadership traits than others from the gene pool of their ancestors. Just as some children are born with talent for music or to run faster than others, some are more naturally gifted with leadership traits like high energy, emotional intelligence, self-confidence, a desire to lead, and the capacity to communicate well. Although many of these leadership characteristics can be developed and are affected positively or negatively by environmental factors, some people have an advantage because of their heritage.

Second, there are *life experiences*. The genetic blueprint of parents impacts an individual's leadership potential, but the environment in which that individual grows during puberty and adolescence also helps determine which behavior patterns actually emerge and are reinforced over time. In many respects, the parent is the primary leadership model that influences a child on how to make sense of experiences, how to understand and treat others, and how to persevere under challenging conditions. Similarly, studies show that an adolescent's self-esteem within a social environment or the ability to master painful conflict during one's developmental years can significantly impact his or her future capacity for leadership.[2] Life experiences can have a big impact on later attempts to develop the leader.

Finally, *intentional cultivation* plays an important role in leadership emergence. Depending on critical influences in a young person's genetic makeup and life experiences, the effectiveness of cultivation can be either optimized or hindered. For example, if a young woman has natural leadership qualities and has been raised in a healthy home environment, the likelihood of her becoming a high-impact leader through good leadership development is quite high. Conversely, one who has been traumatized during puberty or adolescence will have more barriers to overcome in her development process before she can become an effective leader.

It is within this third component of leadership emergence that the more narrow term, leadership development, is found. As an adolescent enters and continues into adulthood, the effort to optimize inherited traits and life experiences by cultivating the individual's leadership capacity to its full potential is what we refer to as "leadership development."

Defining Leadership Development

Leadership development, which is a subset of leadership emergence, can be defined as *adult-focused, intentional cultivation that seeks to establish and enhance effective leadership practices.*

The following points will be helpful to remember.

The above definition implies that leadership development focuses on adults. Certainly there are commendable efforts aimed at broadening the definition to include initiatives for youth, but those initiatives are better defined within the broader realm of leadership emergence. Youth have not had sufficient developmental life experiences to fully engage in adult leadership development.

For the purposes of developing Christ-centered leaders, the desired leadership practices are to be Christ-centered. Therefore, a more precise definition would be *adult-focused intentional cultivation that seeks to establish and enhance effective Christ-centered leadership practices.*

With regard to Christ-centered leadership development, it is good to be reminded that God superintends the emergence of leaders and that He is the ultimate developer of Christ-centered leaders. As we will see in Part Three, our role in intentional cultivation is to plant, water, and nurture emerging leaders with confidence that God will produce positive results in His time. This reminder is both instructive and encouraging as we seek to be instruments of change while recognizing our limitations in the lives of others.

As those who are committed to cultivating effective Christ-centered leadership, our ultimate example is Jesus. He entered this wounded world purposefully and charted a path to impact those who would share His compassion for people and His commitment to serve them. Jesus lived in real time, between the *now* and the *not-yet* of the kingdom. He voluntarily experienced the limitations of humanity, yet He completed His work and bids us complete ours.

Even as we follow Jesus' example and teaching to cultivate leaders, we square it with the reality that we cannot take the place of Jesus in anyone's life, a truth Bishop Ken Untener has so eloquently expressed:

> We cannot do everything, and there is a sense of liberation in that. This enables us to do something and to do it well. It may be incomplete but it is a beginning, a step along the way. . . . We may never see the end results, but that is the difference between the Master Builder and the worker. We are workers, not master builders, ministers not messiahs. We are prophets of a future not our own.[3]

COMPREHENSIVE LEADERSHIP DEVELOPMENT: SIZING UP THE TASK

Picture in your mind's eye an emerging leader you know. As you think about him or her becoming all that God wants them to be, what will it take? What will be needed to make it happen? Answering these questions helps us to get a better idea of the enormity of the challenge.

In conversation with a capable Christian leader, I asked, "If you could assign a dollar figure to the investment of others' time and energy into your own leadership development throughout the years, what would be the cost?"

"How can I estimate the cost?" he replied. "It has been priceless."

This heartfelt response is an indication of the size of the task in leadership development.

If the ultimate goal of our intentional cultivation is "to establish and enhance effective Christ-centered leadership practices," then what components should make up this discipline? What categories of development are essential in the process of cultivating leaders?

There are at least four categories of development that every aspiring Christ-centered leader needs.

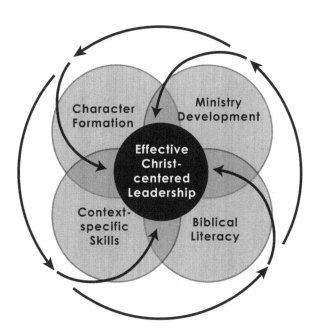

Character Formation

First, character formation is foundational for Christ-centered leadership. It is non-negotiable, for it makes leadership that is Christ-centered possible. Character formation addresses topics such as integrity, honesty, credibility, the spiritual disciplines, and relationships. It also deals with essential issues such as justice, the leadership posture that treats people fairly and equitably.

A few months ago, Mark contacted me on behalf of his church leadership team. His colleague Ed is a skilled leader. After an excellent education at his denomination's seminary, Ed was confirmed for ministry and began serving in their local church. Ed has a vision for a local congregation that reaches across the generational spectrum of modern and postmodern people. He has poured his energy into the work for seven years, and the ministry has experienced significant growth under his leadership. Ed is a capable teacher, a sound theologian, and is adept at many of the duties necessary for leadership. Perhaps this is why few took notice when *eleven* staff members had come and gone in those seven years.

Mark mentioned that over time Ed has become increasingly difficult to work with. When church members question his decisions, he often resorts to temper tantrums. He has chastised lay leaders in front of others for their supposed lack of commitment to the cause. It seems that somewhere along the line his character formation has been shortchanged. The situation has now reached a boiling point, and Ed's future is in jeopardy.

Sadly, many churches deal with a leader who demonstrates commendable skills but questionable character. Skills are to be appreciated and affirmed, but it is imperative that leadership be grounded in godly character. Leadership development without character formation is like building a castle on a stretch of sand; there is nothing to stand on when the storm winds blow and the waters rise. Too few ministry leaders are finishing well, and the problem can often be traced back to character defects. Formation of leadership character is indispensable.

Biblical Literacy

A second category that needs attention is biblical literacy. It goes without saying that effective, Christ-centered leadership must be founded on the Word of God. A firm grasp of the Scriptures, their trustworthiness, and their authority is essential. Christ-centered leaders in storycentric communities must have an applied knowledge of essential doctrines such as the Trinity, sin, redemption, and the church. Additionally, they and the people they lead should also benefit from a healthy understanding of the important events of Christian history, without which today's leaders are in danger of repeating yesterday's mistakes.

Context-specific Skills

Character formation and biblical literacy are of vital importance, but we must build upon their foundation. The third category that needs concerted focus is context-specific skills.

When asked about the qualities people look for in a leader, the vast majority will identify skill competency high on the list. While there are common elements and qualities across the discipline of leadership development, every leader functions in a particular ministry setting that calls for *a specific set* of skills. For example, the pastoral role requires the ability to communicate publicly, to counsel wisely, and to conduct weddings and funeral services. On the other hand, a financial officer of a faith-based charity has to be adept at administration, reading spreadsheets, and planning budgets. The leader of a mission must be good at mingling with the public and generating public interest in the ministry's purpose. Additionally, all these roles are worked out in a *specific cultural context*, which demands interpretation and application of leadership to address actual people in actual places. For example, conflict resolution and the application of peacemaking skills often look different in a shame-based culture than they do in the Western world.

These are just a few examples of the specific skill sets necessary for leaders. The skills can vary widely depending on the ministry context, but regardless of the line of work, leaders need to master specific functions to be effective.

Richard came to faith while an officer in the Navy. Taking an early retirement, he entered seminary to prepare for ministry. Richard poured himself into his studies and did very well. Upon graduation, he had the opportunity to serve on the staff of a large local church. One of his duties was to teach an adult Sunday school class. The class loved his teaching. After a couple of years, the church leadership encouraged him to pastor his own church. Another congregation called him, but he lasted less than two years. The people also enjoyed his teaching but little else. He lacked the people skills to counsel effectively, to lead the various congregational factions in a common direction, or to even provide a modicum of guidance. He left the pastoral ministry feeling defeated. It was only when he accepted a position at a Bible college that Richard came into his own. He realized that he was made to study and to teach. Today, he continues to leverage his leadership influence in the classroom.

Ministry Development

The fourth category is ministry development. Whether leading a house church for nonliterates or serving as president of a Western seminary, ministry development is vital. Leaders need the competencies to serve the organizational aspects of their respective ministries toward healthy growth and progress. Crafting a Christ-centered ministry culture, leading healthy change, communicating well, mentoring effectively, peacemaking, stewarding resources, leading teams, leading strategically, and spiritual leadership are among the essential organizational competencies that effective, Christ-centered leaders need to master.

It is noteworthy that these four categories are not mutually exclusive; one category tends to blend into the others. For example, what a leader understands about the church (biblical literacy) significantly impacts the leader's approach to leading change (ministry development). Development in one category affects development in other categories.

Every emerging candidate for Christ-centered leadership needs development in *all* of these categories to be effective in their ministry role. For example, my Bible college and seminary experience provided excellent development in biblical literacy and some context-specific skills, but a skilled mentor and other non-formal development opportunities were also essential developmental factors. If the leader is exposed to a generous blend of character formation, biblical literacy, context-specific skills, and ministry development, then he or she will likely have greater leadership satisfaction, and the ministry will benefit.

MISTAKING THE PART FOR THE WHOLE

But here's the caveat. While every emerging Christ-centered leader needs all four of these categories to be truly effective, no single school or service provider is proficient to develop leaders effectively in all four categories.

Leadership effectiveness today is hampered by leadership development approaches that mistake a part for the whole. Emerging leaders typically receive development in some of the categories outlined above, but other categories are often overlooked or ignored. This oversight stymies leadership effectiveness, and negatively impacts ministry effectiveness.

You've probably heard the story about the Blind Men and the Elephant. Purported to have originated in India, it has been published in many books for adults and children. In the nineteenth century, the English poet John Godfrey Saxe created the following version:

> It was six men of Indostan
> To learning much inclined,
> Who went to see the elephant
> Though all of them were blind,
> That each by observation
> Might satisfy his mind.

As the poem continues, the blind men variously conclude that the elephant is like a wall, a snake, a spear, a tree, a fan, and a rope, all depending upon which part of the elephant they touch. Saxe's poem concludes:

And so these men of Indostan
Disputed loud and long,
Each in his own opinion
Exceeding stiff and strong,
Though each was partly in the right,
And all were in the wrong!

This parable has been used through the centuries primarily to teach religious and social tolerance. In the Buddhist version, the blind men cannot agree with one another and come to blows over the question of what the elephant is like. The story ends by comparing the blind men to religious leaders and scholars who blindly and ignorantly hold to their own views.

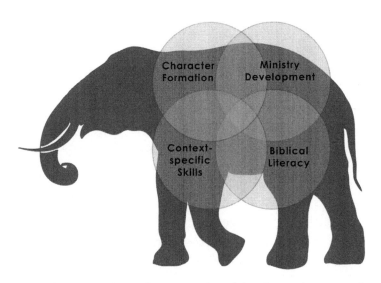

Comprehensive Leadership Development

By applying this analogy to leadership, let's assume that the "elephant" is the discipline of cultivating leaders. And if the whole picture of this elephant—the discipline of cultivating leaders—is intended to "establish and enhance effective, Christ-centered leadership practices," then emerging leaders need a comprehensive developmental approach. This means that all four categories described above—character formation, biblical literacy, context-specific skills, and ministry development—are essential, not just one or two of them.

Hundreds of initiatives worldwide aim to develop Christian leaders. While no single provider is developing leaders effectively in all four categories, many of these providers are doing a commendable job of cultivating leaders effectively in one or two of these categories. For example, seminaries and Bible colleges usually excel at equipping leaders in the areas of theology, doctrine, and church history (biblical literacy) as well as some preaching and pastoral counseling (context-specific skills), but they rarely emphasize the leadership competencies associated with ministry development. Conversely, a vast number of non-formal leadership development entities focus on character formation, but they are not usually equipped to deliver the expertise in the classic leadership disciplines that seminaries provide. This is not a problem as long as these developmental entities recognize their limitations and the need to cooperate with others that specialize in the other developmental categories. However, there is a *big* problem when providers compete with one another and "blindly" function as though their developmental program addresses the whole elephant. As a result, emerging leaders, the ministries they lead, and the people who follow them all suffer the consequences.

Ben has struggled as a leader due to the current environment of ministry leadership development that often mistakes the part for the whole. Ben graduated with a degree in sacred music from a reputable Christian liberal arts university. His college professors were excellent at teaching liberal arts subjects and music theory from a Christian worldview, and he was pleased with his education. He is also a competent musician and an accomplished pianist. A local church was so impressed when Ben showcased his talent during a weekend visit that they offered him a job on the spot. He became their first worship pastor. That was two years ago.

For Ben, the beginning months with the congregation were like a dream come true. The congregation couldn't get enough of his music. The deacons even suggested that he cut a CD of his music to distribute to church visitors. Every Thursday the senior pastor gave him the sermon topic for the week and even offered a few tips on putting together the worship service. "This is easy enough," Ben told himself. "I can put together twenty minutes of songs with a couple of prayers and a few nice transitions for Sunday morning services. This worship ministry is a great gig."

But after the honeymoon period, some of the church members began to long for more of the familiar songs of the past. As Ben entered his fourth month, he faced his first crisis. Two members of the worship team questioned his song selections. They said that most of the songs were new to the congregation, who preferred some of the traditional standards. Ben got into a squabble with these lay volunteers. He reminded them that he was the staff professional and that he would make the decisions. The next Sunday the congregation sang the songs Ben selected, but without a drummer and bass player.

From that day forward, Ben seemed to be embroiled in heated discussions with worship team members on a regular basis. Sometimes the conflict got so heated that they stopped speaking to each other. It was especially awkward when tempers flared just before a Sunday service. Sometimes Ben had to say to the worship team, "I don't care how we are feeling toward one another. Right now we have to perform." So they would put on happy faces and led the congregation in upbeat worship songs and selected Bible verses. It was a miserable experience. Soon the participation of team members became like a revolving door. Keeping the same people on the platform from week to week was almost impossible.

"I can put together a decent worship service," Ben thinks, "but something big is missing. The senior pastor doesn't offer much help. What in the world is the problem?" He is currently brushing up his resume.

Ben's ministry is a result of the "mistaking a part for the whole" syndrome in developing leaders. Knowing good theology and putting together a worship service are important, but pastoring people, both with musical excellence and with leadership maturity, is something Shane did not learn. He can articulate a theology of worship, and his technical skills are more than adequate, but Shane has not yet received the comprehensive package that includes people skills and leading others effectively through change.

A host of younger emerging leaders like Shane are on the losing end of a developmental system perpetuated by leadership development providers who cannot see or will not acknowledge the whole "elephant." This faulty perspective occurs all too frequently. Our well-intentioned efforts to cultivate Christian leaders get hijacked by the quest to satisfy our own success needs rather than the needs of the emerging leaders whom we are commanded and committed to serve. The discipline of leadership development is in desperate want of more collaborative efforts to provide a comprehensive development package so that the emerging generation can become both effective and Christ-centered in their leadership.

CHAPTER 5 SUMMARY

- Leadership development has not been defined well; therefore, the majority of programs aimed to develop ministry leaders are unregulated, lack informed guidance, and have a short shelf life.
- Competent Christ-centered leadership requires development in four overlapping spheres: (1) character formation, (2) biblical literacy, (3) context-specific skills, and (4) ministry development.
- Leadership effectiveness today is hindered by leadership development approaches that mistake a part for the whole.
- No current leadership development initiative effectively provides development all four spheres needed to cultivate competent, Christ-centered leaders; therefore, service providers need to understand the comprehensive need and to partner together so that emerging storycentric leaders are served well to become faithful and effective in their leadership roles.

6
THE PROCESS OF LEADERSHIP DEVELOPMENT

Just six weeks after my conversion experience, I found myself at Toccoa Falls College, a small Christian liberal arts college in northeast Georgia. Their motto is "Where character is developed with intellect." I chose theology as my major, and the professors did stretch me intellectually. My character, on the other hand, was forged primarily on the basketball court. I was far more spiritual in chapel than I was when a guy had his elbow buried in my ribs. On the court, I faced my real self, and sometimes it wasn't pretty. Through my four years on the hardwoods, coaches invested in me every day. Their patience was extraordinary. Both the classroom and the gym had a big impact on my personal and spiritual development.

After graduation, I was ready for ministry! I had studied Bible and theology, ministry and preaching, but for some reason no church offered me a job. With few options, I opted to continue my studies. My new bride, Tina, and I set off for Columbia Biblical Seminary with aspirations to complete more degrees.

In my second year at Columbia, I was eager to demonstrate how much I knew. I found a small rural church in a quaint farming community seventy miles away and convinced the members that they needed a weekend pastor. They yielded and I began with great expectations. Every Sunday I would deliver biblical treatises sprinkled with learned reference to the original languages. I was proud of my sermons—but my listeners were underwhelmed. The congregation "grew" from fifty to thirty and finally to only twenty people.

After two years as weekend pastor, the church board decided (without informing me) to host a week of "revival" services. They invited an evangelist for their special series of meetings. The evangelist had little formal education. He certainly didn't go to Bible school, nor did he know Greek and Hebrew. But he did speak the farmers' language, and he understood their needs. During the meetings, some of the most resistant people made decisions to follow Christ. These special meetings became the talk of their small town. The services were extended from one week to two and then to three. In frustration, I resigned my position as pastor. The evangelist became the pastor, and the church developed a healthy witness in the community.

This initial ministry meltdown made me reluctant to take up church leadership as a vocation. Tina and I decided to pursue another career path instead. However, two weeks before graduation from seminary, a pastor whom I had never met phoned to say he was looking for an assistant. Still bruised from my previous pastoral experience, I responded, "Thank you, but I'm NOT interested."

However, Pastor David Muir was not to be dismissed so easily. "Why don't you just come to visit for the weekend?" he insisted. So I did—but ever so reluctantly.

During the visit, Pastor David heard my story, and said something I will never forget. "Rick, you've been through a tough experience and you seem teachable now. If you'll come to be our assistant pastor, it won't be for what you can do for this church. It will be for what we can do for you."

That was like music to my ears, and of course I said yes! For the next three years, as I served as Pastor David's assistant, he shared his life and leadership lessons with me. He freely offered his wisdom and resources. He believed in me and challenged me. He was committed to my highest kingdom potential. Combined with seminary training, this life-on-life experience in a real ministry setting profoundly changed me and prepared me for future leadership.

Since this pivotal encounter with Pastor David, I have spent my life in various ministry leadership roles, and have had the opportunity to observe what is happening around the world to develop ministry and marketplace leaders in both literate and storycentric communities. My interest and involvement in developing leaders has grown steadily through the decades, and I continue to ask the questions: How do emerging leaders actually grow? What common factors cause real change both in literate and storycentric cultures? What kinds of leadership development are truly effective? How can we get the most return for our investment?

Ministries are making herculean efforts to grow leaders, spending billions of dollars in this pursuit, but is there any real evidence that progress is being made? Interventions to cultivate leaders are absorbing enormous resources, but what does it take for the "leadership" seed to flourish? Jay Conger, Chairman of Leadership Studies at Claremont McKenna College, asks the same question. He wrote, "Despite the attention and money spent [on leadership development] surprisingly few attempts have been made to answer these important questions."[1] These questions deserve more than feel-good answers. That is why, as we develop methods to cultivate leaders in storycentric cultures, we must understand leadership development principles that achieve proven results.

ELEMENTS OF LEADERSHIP DEVELOPMENT

One of the first questions to ask when tackling the issue of developing storycentric leaders is, What primary building blocks are essential if leadership development is to be effective?

While various kinds of leadership development experiences are numerous, most researchers acknowledge that three elements are necessary for any such experience to be effective: feedback, challenge, and support.

Feedback

Feedback within leadership development experiences provides relevant information to the emerging leaders regarding their current leadership strengths, effectiveness, and needs. Good feedback provides clues about how to close the gap between the emerging leaders' current competencies and their required competencies. People's views of themselves are often narrow and naturally biased. The enhanced self-awareness gained through feedback from multiple credible sources is a reliable means to help these emerging leaders know where to focus their developmental efforts. In fact, the collective perception of others is usually more closely aligned with reality than is one's self-perception. Therefore, by motivating leaders to capitalize on their strengths and improve their weaknesses, feedback experiences help them avoid blind spots that can lead to derailment.

Feedback can be formal or informal. Leaders can obtain the desired feedback by a structured means of appraisal that solicits evaluation and recommendations from people with whom the leader works, and often even those in the community. Feedback can also be more informal from friends and trusted colleagues.

Feedback can also work well in storycentric, shame-based cultures. In these communities, the most helpful feedback is usually obtained through casual conversations after a relationship with the evaluator has been established.

When the feedback is presented as a growth opportunity, and when the person receiving it has the ability to appropriately engage or even stop the process, the fear of losing control or being exposed is minimal.

When I worked as a new leader under Pastor David, on many Monday mornings he would provide feedback about my teaching efforts the day before. This continual encounter was pivotal to my growth as a leader. During one memorable feedback session, Pastor David said to me, "Your teaching content was good, and your outline was well-structured, but what were you actually trying to say?" His feedback deeply impacted my teaching. It inspired me to make clear my big idea when communicating with an audience.

On other occasions, I have been given strength inventories or behavioral surveys, to assess my strengths and to better understand my areas of needed growth. It is often enlightening to compare how I view myself with how others view me. Feedback is essential for a meaningful developmental experience.

Challenge

Not only do emerging leaders need feedback; they also need challenging experiences to enable them to change and grow. Effective leadership development often occurs in an environment of disruption that pushes inexperienced leaders out of their comfort zone and causes them to question the adequacy of their current ideas, skills, and approaches. Common sources of challenge are new leadership responsibilities, conflicted relationships, managing people over whom the emerging leader has no delegated authority, and hardship. Challenge serves the dual purpose of motivating leadership development and providing the opportunity for the leader's growth.

During my second year as his assistant, Pastor David appointed me to lead the congregation's Missions Festival. This annual festival was a major event on the church's calendar and required me to coordinate scores of volunteers and guest speakers. At the same time, our second child was due to be born, so you could probably say I was way over my head and way out of my comfort zone. However, I learned invaluable lessons during that experience about my need for leadership growth, and I developed new leadership competencies amid the pressure of real ministry challenges.

Support

Feedback is important, and challenging experiences help us grow, but continual support is also a crucial component of effective leadership development. Leadership development that makes a difference provides confirmation and clarification of lessons learned by the emerging leader. While challenge creates the disequilibrium needed to motivate the emerging leader to change, support from an established leader sends the message that the emerging leader's labor to learn and grow is worth the effort. Support serves as the social cue that attaches a positive interpretation to the emerging leader's struggle as he or she grows and develops.

On the concluding night of the church's Mission Festival—a week in which Tina also gave birth to our son—Pastor David invited me into his office. After we had debriefed the week, he said, "You are becoming a better leader. You juggled your personal responsibilities and the challenges of leading the Festival. I know it was a big deal for you, but you did well." His regular affirmation was an important facet in our mentoring relationship. It not only was encouraging but also genuine and sincere. His "attaboys" encouraged me to stay the course even when the path to leadership growth was long and sometimes difficult.

Feedback, Challenge, and Support: A Three-legged Stool

Effective leadership development experiences are composed of the elements of feedback, challenge, and support—all working together. These elements function like the legs on a three-legged stool. If one leg is removed, then the stool does not stand. Challenge and support without feedback hinders the young leader's self-awareness regarding his or her leadership strengths and areas of needed improvement. Support and feedback without challenge promotes complacency and do not provide the environment of discomfort that is necessary for leadership growth. Challenge and feedback without support often results in discouragement and can stall the emerging leader's developmental progress. Real leadership development is often slow and painful, so generous doses of sincere encouragement are critical for the journey. Leadership development that provides consistent assessment, challenge, and support to the emerging leader has much higher potential for significant positive change in the leader's thinking, values, and behavior.

I recall with great clarity when someone else provided me with the life-changing combination of feedback, challenge, and support. It did not happen in my boss's office, or even in a leadership development classroom. It was a gift delivered over time by my golfing buddy.

I met Peter while pastoring a church outside New York City in the early 1990s. He and his wife, Carolyn, attended the church and dutifully listened to my weekly sermons. Peter and I had breakfast together every other week and played golf as often as we could. Those were the moments during which I would ask for Peter's help on my latest ministry challenges. He was a well-paid communications coach for senior executives in Manhattan, so I felt privileged to have him as my personal confidant.

In those days, as a young and ambitious pastor, I was determined to grow the church. I boldly introduced new approaches that attracted a lot of newcomers, but conflict was ever-present with some of the established parishioners. Congregational meetings were highly charged as I often exerted a strong hand to ensure that the church stayed on course with its mission. Tension mounted.

On one fateful morning, Peter and I were in our usual corner of the café with coffee and muffins. I asked him what he thought was going wrong in the church and if he could suggest what I should do to improve the increasing stress.

"Rick, you speak pretty well and are a forceful leader," he replied. "But you consistently seem to want to top what people have to say, to prove something to them. You're like a bull trying to dominate the herd. You are a poor listener."

I had assumed that Peter would take my side and say that others were the problem, so his answer naturally felt like a solid blast. Later that day, wanting to test Peter's analysis, I asked my wife if she thought I was a poor listener.

"Honey, I love you," responded Tina kindly, "but yes, you're a lousy listener."

That was not what I wanted to hear, and it was definitely not a view of myself that I cherished—argumentative, bullheaded, trampling on other people. It was hard to accept, but I had to consider the input very seriously, since both Peter and Tina said it was so. I was faced directly with a contradiction between what I believed about myself and what others saw in me. It was like living in a hall of mirrors: there was no hiding from the reflections they gave me of myself.

Two weeks later, I met with Peter again. I told him about the conversation with Tina and expressed my need for help to become a better listener. I am very grateful that instead of turning me away Peter said, "I'll help you to become a better listener."

For the next two years, he gave me challenging assignments to improve my listening. I could always trust him to support me and to provide honest feedback about my progress. Sometimes Peter would compliment me for exhibiting good listening in a public setting, and other times he would point out ways I could listen better. The journey was sometimes quite difficult, but it was ultimately transformational. Today Tina assures me that I am a better listener (although I still have occasional lapses), and the impact upon my leading others has been encouraging.

My story is not unique. We probably all have stories that affirm the importance of feedback, challenge, and support as essential elements for effective leadership development.

But while the elements of feedback, challenge, and support have the potential for positive change in the leader's thinking, values, and behavior, certain questions remain. For instance, to what extent do these elements impact the people that the leader actually leads? Leadership development is not just about the leader; it is also about the ultimate impact on the lives of those who follow. Furthermore, are some types of leadership experiences more effective than others?

TYPES OF LEADERSHIP DEVELOPMENT EXPERIENCES

Virtually all leadership development research affirms the importance of the elements of feedback, challenge, and support, but confusion prevails as to what types of experiences are most effective. Many types of experiences develop leadership abilities. A wide range of leadership development experiences can be categorized into the following four types, which are not mutually exclusive: training; experiential learning; developmental relationships; and on-the-job assignments.

Training

An online ad read: "Take your leadership to the next level. Our world-class faculty and trainers help church leaders elevate their leadership. Participants study cutting-edge ideas and come away equipped with the tools of highly effective leaders. You will return to your ministry with confidence and know that you can be a great leader to others!"

This is a promotion for leadership *training*, and it represents the type of leadership development experience that is most readily available for ministry leaders today. The vast majority of leaders go through some form of training during their vocational (and private) lives. It may be formal or informal; short or long; computer-based or instructor-led; literacy-focused or storycentric; and mandatory or voluntary. And it may be passed on through lectures, case studies, or even role-play. Most of us have experienced both good training and not-so-good training. We have encountered training that is very relevant to our leadership, and some that makes us wonder, Why am I here?

Training is a developmental event in which individuals gain knowledge necessary to hone an existing competency and to develop new ones. It is focused on technical or "soft" skills. Since the scope of knowledge that can be learned through training is vast, we are concerned here with the specific knowledge that leaders need.

The context for leadership training can range from a half-day seminar on decision-making to a seminary degree program spanning years. Traditionally, training programs transfer information primarily through conceptual frameworks and abstract principles. However, in more storycentric cultures, training employs the oral arts such as stories, drama, images, and music. In India, for example, training was conducted for twenty semiliterate and nonliterate pastors. As they sat on the cement floor under a tin roof, they learned key leadership principles through hearing selected Gospel narratives. After this presentation, the facilitator engaged the pastors in discussion by asking key questions about the narrative so that the participants "self-discovered" the important principles. After the exercise, the group was divided into four smaller groups. One group was assigned to prepare a drama based upon the biblical narrative. The second group created a cultural drama that taught the lessons learned. A third group drew a picture to depict the leadership principles. And a fourth group worked together to come up with an original song that teaches the biblical truths. After working in smaller groups, the groups presented their dramas, picture, and song in consecutive order. At the conclusion of the session, all the participants locked arms and danced as they sang the original song. This use of repetition served as an effective learning method in storycentric training.

Whether literacy-based or storycentric, effective training concerns itself with two primary objectives: it defines the *idealized* state, and it helps participants identify their *real* state.

First, training defines the idealized state—*how things should be*. Effective leadership training facilitates learning about preferred leadership thinking, attitudes, and behavior. A training event teaches the ideal way that leaders should lead. Whether the learning is about strategic thinking, integrity, creativity, managing conflict, or teamwork, training focuses on the desired competencies associated with effective leadership.

Second, training assists participants to identify their real state— *how things currently are*. The leadership competencies that are taught allow individuals to get a sense of their need for growth by comparing their own current leadership attitudes and practices against the ideal way leaders should lead. A university class typically uses formal testing to accomplish this objective. Nonformal training events, on the other hand, often employ exercises that help participants reflect on their own leadership in light of the desired thinking and behavior.

Training is clearly an important leadership development experience. But is training, in and of itself, enough to produce an effective leader? This is a good question to think about even as we look at the three other types of leadership experiences.

Experiential Learning

I worked for a Christian college in California during the 1990s. The department I led during those years used experiential learning to prepare students for team leadership on their annual cross-cultural missions trips. After the student leaders had studied leadership for several months in small groups, the program's director coordinated a "wilderness trek" into the northern Nevada desert. For six days, these leaders faced the harsh desert elements with a bare minimum of the customary creature comforts (toothbrushes, toilet paper, and shampoo were regarded as contraband). These extreme circumstances provided ideal conditions for students to face the best and worst in themselves and in one another.

One year I tagged along to experience the trek personally. I confess that I was part participant and part observer (in other words, I smuggled toilet paper into my backpack). The coeducational group to which I was assigned was composed of six male students, five female students, and a professional guide. On the first day, we hiked about ten miles.

An hour or so before sunset, the trail had taken us down into a ravine, with massive rock walls on both sides. Without warning we came upon a pool of water that stretched from one side of the ravine to the other. The pool was about thirty feet wide and five feet deep, and there was no way around it. To retreat up and out of the ravine was out of the question; the only logical path was forward. But that was when we learned that one of the students could not swim. She began to lose her composure in fear of the pool's dark water. The guide and I stood back to observe how the students would deal with their first major challenge.

One of the young men decided to show off his surging testosterone at this moment. Throwing caution aside, he jumped into the water with backpack overhead and began to wade through the frigid water. As he reached the other side, he had to climb onto a huge rock to get out of the pool. He tried to step onto the slimy rock while holding his pack overhead with both hands. As a result, he lost his footing and did a face plant right onto the rock. We all watched helplessly from the other side as blood poured from his nose and chin. Every ounce of his macho demeanor drained away as he fought back the tears.

Eventually the others came up with a solution. They formed a human chain across the pool, passed the backpacks from one person to another, and finally helped their frightened friend who could not swim to the other side. As soon as everyone had safely navigated the pool, the sun went behind the mountain, and the sky opened up with a desert downpour. We pulled a huge tarp over ourselves and endured the night. At sunrise our guide debriefed the experience over coffee as we dried out our clothes and gear. The students learned valuable lessons about leadership that day and in the days that followed.

What has been revived in recent years to prepare leaders in Western society actually dates to centuries past in storycentric contexts. Just as the father takes his young son into the forest to teach him the art of hunting, so experiential learning is a time-tested process in storycentric societies whereby people work and learn together by tackling real issues and reflecting on their actions.

Experiential learning meets the following essential conditions:

- The learner must be a willing and active participant in the experience.
- The learner must reflect on the experience.
- The learner must be able to use decision-making and problem-solving skills to learn from the experience.

Experiential learning includes but is not limited to outdoor learning, ropes courses, action learning, group exercises, and simulations. Participants acquire knowledge through actual actions and practice, which expose their values, preferences, and personalities in a way that traditional instruction cannot do.

Experiential learning is valued because people naturally develop skills in areas that are most comfortable for them. They default to certain ways of overcoming obstacles based on their personalities and past experiences. Leaders naturally rely on their current strengths, yet every leader faces new challenges that require different approaches. As situations change, new development needs surface. Experiential learning is a type of leadership development that uses the tools of action and reflection to help participants maintain awareness of their current leadership strengths while cultivating additional competencies to meet new leadership challenges.

Developmental Relationships

You've probably been at a conference and heard someone tout the value of a mentor. Or you know of a leader who has an executive coach. These points of information may have raised your awareness but they have yet to produce a clear and meaningful picture of a developmental relationship in your mind. You might even become confused or doubtful, wondering whether this is just the latest fad du jour or a form of therapy for leaders. If so, you are not alone in your uncertainty. These kinds of developmental experiences are less known than traditional training or education programs.

Western society's folk heroes like the Lone Ranger have promoted a popular myth that great leaders make it on their own. But a closer look reveals that nothing could be further from the truth—not even for the Lone Ranger. According to legend, six Texas Rangers were ambushed by the Butch Cavendish gang and left for dead. A Native American named Tonto stumbled on the scene and found a lone survivor, John Reid. Tonto nursed Reid back to health, and the two men dug six graves so that the outlaws would think there were no survivors. John Reid then fashioned a black mask to conceal his identity. Along with Tonto, he brought the Cavendish gang to justice. Afterwards, Reid and Tonto continued to fight evil together. People only remember the Lone Ranger today, but had it not been for Tonto, we would have never heard of the Lone Ranger!

Contrary to popular myth, no leader makes significant impact solely on the basis of his or her own talents and efforts. Numerous studies indicate that effective leaders have at least three significant developmental relationships in the course of their lifetimes.

For years Tiger Woods, arguably the world's greatest golfer, relied on swing coach Butch Harmon to elevate and optimize his game. Swimmer Michael Phelps, who has won a record 22 Olympic medals, has coach Bob Bowman. Singer Céline Dion had husband Réne Angélil. Former US Secretary of State Condoleezza Rice gives much of the credit for her leadership acumen to her relationship with her parents.

Speaking about legendary coach Vince Lombardi, football player Jerry Kramer said, "He made us all better than we thought we could be." In the corporate world, chief executives at eBay, Charles Schwab, Pfizer, Maytag, and Ford Motors have all turned to mentors and coaches to improve their leadership.

For Christian leaders, developmental relationships are deeply rooted in biblical principles. In the Old Testament, Joshua looked to Moses for leadership development, Naomi to Ruth, Samuel to Eli, and Elisha to Elijah.

In the New Testament, Barnabas saw potential in Saul (later Paul the Apostle) when others kept their distance. After Saul's conversion from Hebrew henchman to Christian evangelist, most disciples of Jesus feared him and were reluctant to let him attend their potlucks. "But Barnabas took him [Saul] and brought him to the apostles" (Acts 9:27). Barnabas came alongside him and vouched for him. Undoubtedly, Barnabas encouraged and taught Saul during those early days, patiently tolerating his mistakes and abrasiveness. He saw potential and knew that time, experience, and the sanctifying work of the Holy Spirit would temper and mature this gifted leader. Later, Paul paid it forward when he groomed Timothy for ministry leadership. As these examples show, leaders rely on developmental relationships to reach their highest potential to advance the Kingdom of God.

A developmental relationship is first and foremost an *intentional* relationship between two people. While serendipitous relationships can certainly be formational, the developmental relationships to which we refer are almost always intentional. These developmental relationships are not just the result of accidental chemistry but are thoughtfully implemented for promising young recruits as well as mature leaders who want to expand their current competencies.

Such a relationship can come in several forms. Definitions for the various kinds of developmental relationships vary, so here are some simple descriptions:[2]

- A *mentor* provides insight by asking good questions and sharing both life and leadership lessons primarily through his or her experience.
- A *coach* provides confidential, one-on-one partnership that focuses on prescribed, relevant performance enhancement for the participant.
- A *spiritual guide* provides accountability, direction, and discernment regarding God's initiatives in the life and leadership of the participant.
- A *counselor* provides timely advice and correct perspectives on viewing self, others, and circumstances.
- A *teacher* provides knowledge and understanding on a particular topic in a relational context.
- A *sponsor* provides career guidance and advocates for the participant within an organization.

Although participants typically tend to seek a single development relationship that will fulfill the whole range of these functions, they rarely find one that will meet this expectation. However, if a participant is willing to narrow their needs to one or two specific areas, then they are more likely to find someone available to meet that need.

Developmental relationships have been key elements in the continuity of art, craft, commerce, and leadership in storycentric communities for thousands of years. Although mentoring and coaching are making a comeback in Western societies, storycentric communities are more historically attuned to the essential necessity of developmental relationships. In much the same way as skills were passed from generation to generation in the Middle Ages, a young boy in a storycentric village accompanies his father to the village market to learn the skill of bartering. On the other hand, the six-year-old boy in a literacy-based town is sent off to school, where he learns to read about life. His interaction with the teacher is a formal one, generally limited to academic matters. Developmental relationships should play a central role early in a person's life in literacy-based societies, just as they have been an essential function of storycentric cultures for centuries.

We lead in a messy world, where disasters happen, diseases decimate, hopes are crushed, and trust is betrayed. We lead in a world that breaks our hearts if we stick around long enough. But our mentors and coaches hover over us like wings of grace. I am indebted to those who invested in me—Pastor David, my dear friend Colin, and above all, my Dad.

These men formed me while they were alive, and when they died I was compelled to revisit the places they had inhabited in my heart. Through the process, I have discovered a part of me that is each of them. It will never take their place, of course; the loss is still loss, and I feel each man's absence to this day. But my present and future hope have become part of their legacy. These men who went before me are still my mentors, still helping me become who I alone can be.

I did not earn or merit my relationship with them; that was a gift, plain and simple. And beyond the wisdom and knowledge that each man passed on to me, the best gift he gave me was *himself*. My response to a gift this priceless is never-ending gratitude, and to keep my heart and mind open to others I meet along the way. If I can give myself as these men did, I will consider my life well spent.

The leaders of tomorrow are crying out for mentors and coaches. They desperately want more experienced leaders to walk alongside them, to help them discover underused strengths, maintain focus in the midst of hardship, eliminate blind spots, and master new challenges.

Those who are committed to relationships that hone effective leadership thinking, values, and behavior are in great demand, because those with less experience yearn for leaders with more experience who will choose to give of themselves. The emerging generation no longer views developmental relationships as an option. These young leaders regard the investment of mentors and coaches in their lives as a non-negotiable requirement for their effectiveness in the future. Developmental relationships are vital to leadership development. But is having a mentor or being a mentor all that is necessary to develop effective leaders? It's a fair question, but let's look at one last type of leadership development experience before we put it all together.

On-the-Job Assignments

Think about situations in which you've participated in training, experiential learning, and developmental relationships. Now take a few moments and reflect on at least one job (or an assignment that was part of a job) in which you learned a great deal. Ask yourself what it was about this role that was so important in your development.

- Did you have to deal with difficult people?
- Were you expected to coordinate something with which you were unfamiliar?
- Did you need to build a team of people from scratch?
- Was there risk involved?
- Were you responsible to influence people over whom you had no delegated authority?
- What did you learn, and how do you lead differently today because of your experiences in that job?

On-the-job assignments are one of the oldest types of leadership development. They are similar to experiential learning in that on-the-job assignments focus on learning by doing, but they are distinct from experiential learning in that they give the opportunity for emerging leaders to learn in a real-time leadership role. Experiential learning is about creating conditions in which people are pushed outside their comfort zones so they can be stretched. In the end, however, the environment for experiential learning is usually not the actual context where we work and lead, whereas an on-the-job assignment contains actual conditions in which the stakes for success or failure are much higher.

On-the-job assignments require emerging leaders to think and act differently. These types of jobs or ministry assignments often are not well-defined. They present responsibilities that are new and different; they contain problems to solve and require choices to be made under conditions of risk and uncertainty. This type of leadership development experience is intended to teach practical knowledge and skills that expand the young leaders' effectiveness. It places them in a real-time situation that forces them to draw conclusions and apply lessons learned to meet current challenges. Examples of on-the-job assignments include:

- Representing staff concerns to senior management
- Taking on a new position that stretches the emerging leader to develop new abilities
- Dealing with a ministry crisis
- Designing a training course
- Managing a project outside the learner's area of expertise

Ministry organizations usually appoint people to jobs based on their preexisting skills rather than for developmental purposes. However, those that use challenging assignments to groom emerging leaders typically find that these experiences are invaluable both to the young leader and to the organization when they provide growth opportunities through novel experiences, difficult tasks, conflict, and even disappointment. Multiple studies of effective leaders have found that these kinds of assignments were crucial in their development. On-the-job experiences are typically more influential than formal training in leadership development. Let me explain what I mean.

LEADERSHIP DEVELOPMENT THAT REALLY WORKS

We have examined the elements of leadership development experience (*feedback*, *challenge*, and *support*) and the types of leadership development experiences (*training*, *experiential learning*, *developmental relationships*, and *on-the-job assignments*). But some questions still remain: Do any of these types of leadership development really make a difference? And if they do, does one type of leadership development have a bigger impact in changing leadership behavior than another? Are some development experiences better than others in cultivating effective leaders? What development experiences actually result in changed leaders? And how do we measure whether leadership development is actually working?

To find answers to these questions, I conducted PhD dissertation research to find out whether current leadership development efforts are effective.[3] And there is good news.

After hundreds of surveys, scores of interviews, and in-depth data analysis, the verdict is: *Yes, leadership development really does work—but not in the way many assume.* Let's examine how leadership development, properly applied, actually works. Before we do this, however, here are some sober findings.

Sober Findings: Stand-alone Efforts

Most leaders have experienced at least one of the four leadership development types. They have either: attended a leadership seminar (*training*); participated in a leadership retreat (*experiential learning*); had a coach or mentor (*developmental relationship*); or been appointed to a challenging job (*on-the-job assignment*). Some have experienced several of these types of leadership development over the course of their adult lives.

However, the results of my research uncovered objective evidence that many of our current leadership development efforts are not producing the desired results. Most of the respondents had experienced some kind of leadership development, but in many cases it was difficult to determine whether having any type of leadership development was more helpful than having no leadership development at all.

In fact, leaders who had experienced only training scored lower in their leadership evaluations. Some of these leaders had received classroom training on leadership. Others had participated in numerous leadership seminars, but the cumulative impact of this training on their leadership growth was negligible. Although the vast majority of of all Christian leadership development is training, the research revealed that less than ten percent of leaders who experience *only* training demonstrate any lasting change in their leadership. What is the reason for this? Let's look further.

Three factors impact the ineffectiveness of training as a stand-alone leadership development experience. First, training usually happens in a bubble. In other words, it is removed from the day-to-day work experience, both in terms of time and real-world application. Second, training provides knowledge about leadership skills but rarely develops those skills in the leader. Third, the excitement often felt by participants in skill-based training is often short-lived. Leaders who participate in training are eager to apply the learning, but often the enthusiasm dissipates when their new ideas are met with suspicion in the workplace.

Stand-alone training can actually be counterproductive. Imagine your boss announces that she is going to Cancun for two weeks to attend an all-expenses-paid leadership seminar. You and your coworkers are secretly envious that she's off to a luxury resort, but expectations rise in the office that she will return to be a better leader. At the end of two weeks, she returns with new ideas and a fancy three-ringed binder packed with PowerPoint presentations. Initially, she is full of enthusiasm for the new approaches, but in another two weeks, all is back to normal. Nothing changes, and your boss is mostly the same leader as before.

This familiar scenario is an example of training that generates heightened expectations among those led that leadership will get better, but does little to impact the long-term behavior of the leader. As a result, the perception gap between the expectations of the workers and the actual behavior of the leader grows even wider, creating an increased sense of disappointment among the leader's colleagues.

The research further revealed that leaders who experienced only experiential learning also demonstrated relatively little change in their leadership behaviors. Many leaders expressed appreciation for the opportunity to learn from experiences away from the workplace, but as a stand-alone experience this type of leadership development also did not typically result in the desired growth.

A rather surprising result of this research is the relatively insignificant impact of a developmental relationship on a leader's behavior when it is the *only* type of development a leader experiences. Mentoring and coaching have gained much attention in recent years and are used in many contexts and cultures to cultivate leaders. But even these relationships as stand-alone experiences are not as impactful as they purport to be. Although the mentor and the mentee usually perceive their developmental relationship as effective in producing leadership growth, other raters—such as those who work for and with the leader (employees and colleagues)—are less convinced that the developmental relationship results in much significant change in the leader.

So that leaves one category to consider, and here the research reveals some promise. *An on-the-job assignment is the only type of stand-alone leadership development experience that results in observable leadership growth.* Therefore, if pressed to select only one development type that will yield a positive return on investment—for example, when a multipronged plan isn't possible because the budget is tight or expert providers aren't available—then the on-the-job assignment is the best single choice among the available options. Having to choose is far from ideal, as you will see in the following section, but if you have to choose, choose to immerse the emerging leader in a challenging job and hope that he or she survives!

In summary, each of the four types of leadership development experiences is important, but they have limited impact when operating in isolation. Only by working in combination can they produce significant progress in the development of leaders. This combination of types is what might be referred to as "the gold standard."

Encouraging Findings: The Gold Standard

With the exception of on-the-job assignments, all the other types of leadership development as stand-alone experiences are generally ineffective. And even though on-the-job assignments win bragging rights as a *marginally* significant stand-alone developmental experience, the result is also a hit-and-miss proposition: some emerging leaders who take on new assignments are able to overcome the challenges, while others are not. In short, the bad news is that no leadership development type is highly effective as a stand-alone experience to grow better leaders.

But the good news is that this bad news is not the only news! The research uncovered a treasured principle: *the gold standard for leadership development is found in the combination of developmental types.* When working in conjunction with each other, multiple types of leadership development create a potent recipe for significant growth in leaders.

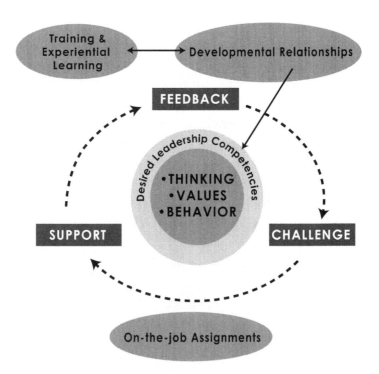

The graph above depicts a process that effectively cultivates desired leadership competencies. Several points from the graph are worth highlighting:

- There is no direct line from training and experiential learning to the desired leadership competencies. Rather, the combination of training and experiential learning along with developmental relationships results in significant observable change in an emerging leader's competencies.
- Ministry organizations experience a higher return on their investment of resources when they shift more of their time and energy from training to providing developmental relationships in the context of a job that stretches the emerging leader's capacity.
- The line between training/experiential learning and developmental relationships points both ways. This bidirectional arrow indicates that a good developmental relationship provides some training and can also be supported by more structured training and experiential learning.

The key takeaway is this: *Training and experiential learning combined with developmental relationships that provide ongoing assessment, challenge, and support delivered on the foundation of on-the-job assignments cultivates effective leaders.* Evidence demonstrates that this model really works to produce the desired change in the leader's thinking, values, and behavior both in literate and in storycentric cultures.

My own leadership journey confirms this idea. My college and seminary experience (*training*) combined with mentoring from Pastor David (*developmental relationship*) as I functioned in a ministry leadership role (*on-the-job assignment*) deeply impacted my leadership thinking, values, and behavior.

Does leadership development actually work? Yes, it absolutely does. But it must be done comprehensively, and there are no shortcuts. Trying to develop leaders on the cheap—for example, running the administrative team through a one-day training seminar or even sending them on a weekend wilderness experience—may provide some marginal benefits in morale or team building. Leadership competencies, however, likely will remain largely unchanged.

As you reflect on your development as a leader, did you have a mentor who provided good feedback, challenge, and support? Was your training supported by developmental relationships and job assignments that challenged you to grow? If so, you received a great blessing, and your leadership today is probably impacted positively. If not, then begin today to seek this kind of leadership development to reach your God-given potential. This is the gold standard for developing effective, leaders today in both literate and storycentric societies.

Here and there in this chapter, we've considered how leadership development principles might be translated into storycentric settings. Now it is time to take this gold standard and begin using it for the preparation of Christ-centered leaders who will advance the kingdom of God.

CHAPTER 6 SUMMARY

- Three elements are essential for a leadership development experience to be effective: (1) feedback, (2) challenge, and (3) support.
- Four types of leadership development have been evaluated for effectiveness: (1) training, (2) experiential learning, (3) development relationships, and (4) on-the-job assignments.
- With the exception of on-the-job assignments, all the other types of leadership development as stand-alone experiences are generally ineffective. Moreover, on-the-job assignments as a stand alone experience are only marginally effective.
- The gold standard for leadership development is found in the combination of developmental types.
- Training and experiential learning combined with developmental relationships that provide ongoing assessment, challenge, and support delivered on the foundation of on-the-job assignments cultivates effective leaders.

PART THREE

Christ-Centered Leadership

7
LEADERSHIP MATTERS

Nelson Mandela. Idi Amin. Golda Meir. Pol Pot. Mother Teresa. Elizabeth Elliott. Bono.

The very mention of these names triggers images of leaders who have shaped the course of people's lives in storycentric contexts. Leaders, both good ones and bad ones, affect each of us. We've all experienced leadership that has impacted us, our loved ones, or our community, and this experience is supported by mounds of evidence dating back to ancient times. Writings like Plato's *Republic*, for instance, reflect how profoundly leaders mark people and cultures. No one escapes the influence of leaders.

Yes, leadership matters. Like everyone else, storycentric communities also long for good leaders. They, too, want to follow leaders who display resolve and grace under pressure, leaders who will give themselves for the good of those they lead. These are all reasons why the leadership that Jesus Christ modeled two thousand years ago is still so appealing during this hour of human history. Regardless of one's culture or religion, people are attracted to Jesus' way of leading.

Robert Greenleaf recounted the story of Rabbi Heschel, a leading Jewish theologian and philosopher of the twentieth century, who was teaching a class of students on the Old Testament prophets.[1] In his lecture, the rabbi spoke of the true prophets and the false prophets. When he finished, a student asked him how one can tell the difference between the true prophet and the false prophet.

"There is no single, proven way," the rabbi answered. "If there was a proven way, if I could establish without question that the prophet is true or false, then there would be no human dilemma, and life would have no meaning."

What Rabbi Heschel said of prophets is also true of Christian leaders. Jesus' leadership has always been admired and romanticized, but it is hard to define and even harder to practice. There is no single way that proves the difference between a leader who is leading like Jesus and one who is not. There is not one standard measuring stick. Yet we can see clear evidence of those who are faithful to Christ in their leadership. And unfortunately, if we dare to look, we will also see the distressing signals of others who are leading poorly.

Thousands around the globe today are diligently reflecting the wonder of Christ through their leadership. God is doing some amazing work in and through these men and women who are committed to honor Christ. Although a few of them are household names, most of them serve in relative obscurity. Yet their collective leadership has altered the course of people and nations. God knows each one of them by name, and their reward will be handsome.

I met one of these leaders on a trip to China some years ago, shortly after the border officials had checked our government-issued documents and approved us for entry. His name was Sebastian, and for the next several days he led us on a whirlwind tour of the church in his beloved homeland. He told us many stories about miracles but also reflected on the personal pain of persecution and suffering.

Sebastian was born into a Christian family in China in the 1930s. He followed in his father's footsteps and became a noted church leader in southern China. As his leadership role became more prominent and public, he faced increasing scrutiny from the Mao authorities. Despite their covert threats, he was unwilling to compromise his commitment to lead an "unregistered" church. He was eventually arrested and imprisoned for twenty-three years in a labor camp, being finally released at the age of sixty-seven. Sebastian was faithful to his leadership calling. "Although I forfeited my prominent pastoral post," he told us with a sense of satisfaction, "the church in China today is flourishing."

"Bud" Hancock is another leader who leads like "Jesus with skin on." In the 1980s, Bud worked in the Reagan administration, and he has since served in several high-profile roles in both the public and private sectors. He has repeatedly spoken out with clarity on principled matters, even when his position is unpopular. At times he has been marginalized for his biblical convictions, only to be exonerated when the truth was eventually exposed.

Bud is also a serial entrepreneur. He has taken great delight over the years to entrust the leadership reigns of organizations he started into the care of a capable younger generation. He consistently extends mercy in massive supply to others. For the past decade or so Bud has been running a program for parolees of the California State prison system to help former inmates become fulfilled and fruitful citizens, and to reduce the number of those who return to prison. Bud is a leader who will give others the shirt off his back. I know, because he provided moral and spiritual support to me during a rough patch in my ministry career.

God is being glorified by leaders like Bud and Sebastian, who are faithful in their diverse vocations. They serve in contexts that are healthy and growing, not simply in numbers, but especially in Christian maturity and spirituality.

The challenges of Christian leadership are as acute today as at any time since the days of Jesus. Whether a leader lives in an environment that is overtly hostile to the gospel or in one that is more sympathetic to Christian witness, these faithful ones demonstrate that serving Jesus by leading others involves more than the ability to communicate well, author books, or attract a host of admirers. They remind us of witnesses through the centuries who have lived and led for Christ with wholehearted devotion. Those who have gone before us, as well as those who serve alongside us in the present, inspire us to seek the reality of God in our leadership until we pass the torch to future generations.

However, there are also troubling indicators, and the credibility of many Christian leaders is sadly compromised. While some exemplify both integrity and effectiveness, others' lives and leadership cast a foreboding shadow. We all know some of these people.

A young leader from the Middle East described his experience this way: "I work with a small Christian mission in my country. We face security risks every day. The leader of our mission recently read a book written by a well-known Christian leader from America that teaches principles for success. Our senior leader is trying to practice the lessons from the book, but the lessons are tempting us to be successful through compromise rather than faithfulness to Christ. What does 'success' mean for Christian ministries in our nation?"

At the risk of over-generalizing, the quest for success in the West and the quest for honor in the Majority World are negatively impacting a vast multitude of Christian leaders and the ministries they lead. Being fruitful in ministry has been redefined by these terms.

The intoxicating lure of success causes many admiring followers to gloss over a leader's character lapses in lieu of idolizing his or her productivity. Examples abound of Christian leaders who are successful by secular measures, but their leadership resembles the world's more than that of Jesus. In nearly every community on earth, ministry leaders can be found who imitate the prevailing power model of leadership in their respective cultures. Too often Christian leaders are recognizable more for their status, rank, and honor than for their character. To perpetuate this charade, they often end up prioritizing image over genuine health. These leaders and those who follow them are high on the numbing effects of personal and professional success.

A Christian worker in India was distressed because his ministry supervisor evaluated him on the number of people he baptized in a given month. If the numbers were up, then he was praised. If the numbers were down, then he was sharply reprimanded. The idea of success determined by numbers was drilled into his psyche in training seminars on evangelism and church growth. During staff meetings, reports of baptisms determined the latest pecking order. The pressure to produce more and more eventually drove him out of the organization, but the good news is that his departure forced him to reexamine his ministry with fresh eyes to see how God wanted him to go about it.

THE QUEST FOR SUCCESS

Success is not inherently wrong; healthy growth is a good thing. People, communities, and organizations that are not experiencing progress and growth are usually in trouble.

I grew up in Cary, in eastern North Carolina. When my family moved to Cary in 1959, there were about 3,000 people and one stoplight. Ashworth's Drugs was our pharmacy and the main lunch counter open to blue- and white-collar workers alike. As a boy, I enjoyed riding my bike downtown, and chasing chickens at Kildare Farm. Most people knew "Ricky," so Dad usually got wind of my shenanigans before sundown.

Although I have been all over the world, I once again live off of Kildare Farm Road, now a multi-lane thoroughfare that runs through the heart of Cary. Where the farm once was, a shopping center has been built. Condominiums have sprung up where tobacco once grew. A mall now sits on our former baseball field. The cozy town where I grew up is now the seventh largest city in North Carolina, home to more than 145,000 people. Most residents are "outsiders" who work in the Research Triangle, headquarters for more than 170 global companies including IBM, Syngenta, Credit Suisse, and Cisco. Most of them don't know the Cary of my youth. Still, I'm grateful that the growth has provided a hospital, a world-class gym, and hundreds of fine eateries within minutes of my place. I'm also glad that people from almost every culture and religion now call Cary their home.

To me, the healthy progress of the city of Cary is a good thing. But when the quest for "success" overshadows "health" it is easy to lose our way.

Every leader wants to be part of something that is robust and fruitful. No leader wants to fail. To be called a failure is considered a damning indictment. There is a desire within each of us to be seen and appreciated and to have security and significance. When all is said and done, we want to be valued and loved. It tastes sweet to have success, to be promoted, and to be esteemed.

But like cotton candy, the sweet taste of success does little for our souls. In a distorted world where people are in constant competition with one another, the quest to outdo the next guy is firmly entrenched in the human heart. Leaders resort to power and control to make things happen. They may say that people are the organization's most valuable resource, but they often prioritize the success of the organization at the expense of people. Patricia and Mike learned this the hard way.

Patricia grew up as a missionary kid in Latin America, Mike was from a stable and loving home in Michigan. They met in college, fell in love, and got married. Early in their careers, both Mike and Patricia were recognized for their leadership ability. Mike became a junior executive. Patricia advanced in healthcare management. They both earned substantial salaries.

It wasn't long before Patricia and Mike had two children, a beautiful home, and were living the American dream. But they were restless. They wanted to give themselves to a cause they could believe in. So they signed up with a Christian mission and sold their home, their vehicles, and most of their belongings. They packed what was left into a few suitcases and moved to the Caribbean as missionaries.

Due to their leadership ability and potential, Mike became the mission's Director of Operations with Patricia by his side. But in time they began to notice some serious problems within the organization, clinging to it like ugly barnacles on the hull of a ship. Senior leaders ran the mission like a business; they were more interested in productivity than ministry to people. Patricia and Mike had joined the ministry organization with the assumption that practicing Jesus' way of leadership would be championed and celebrated. Instead, they got trapped in major conflict with "big boss" senior leaders. For three years they tried to navigate the turbulence that whirled in their mission relationships. But their effort to reconcile the inconsistencies led to disillusionment. They eventually resigned their ministry positions and returned to secular work, where they felt they could have more of a Christian influence.

Many like Mike and Patricia have been willing to forsake all to work with Christian ministries, but they encounter a leadership approach that doesn't remind them of Jesus. In their well-intentioned attempts to challenge these prominent "ministry" leadership models, they face the negative consequence of overwhelming political forces at play in these ministries.

Christian leaders today often function with a leadership paradigm that prioritizes success above everything else. Too many leaders and their organizations operate under the guise of "fruitful ministry" that is defined by numbers and budgets. Having defined success by these dubious secular standards, the leaders are then touted as icons to be admired and copied. Books by and about them are offered as how-to manuals for those with ministry aspirations. As a result of such pseudo-ministry leadership models, both the leaders and their followers ultimately lose a clear focus on Christ-centered living and leading.

Without thoughtful reflection, leadership success has become the dominant cultural preference among ministry leaders. These leaders unwittingly prioritize success above all else. Why do we really count the number of people in the congregation on Sunday? Why do we really ask others how many people are in their church? Have we equated numbers with effectiveness? Some pastors privately confess that hearing a story of another struggling local pastor gives them secret feelings of joy and satisfaction. Although they are shamed by their admission and recognition of it, such an attitude is understandable when the idea of success by numbers has been drilled into our minds. When success is primarily about numbers or size, we can expect a destructive, competitive spirit even among Christian leaders.

In like fashion, boards of Christian organizations typically evaluate their senior executives primarily on their ability to raise funds and expand the ministry's footprint. Over time, while the notion of spiritual leadership might still be given lip service, in reality Christ-centered leadership is eclipsed by the preference for a Chief Executive Officer. Since success is the predominant measurement for leadership, ambitious leaders in Christian organizations function on the premise that the ultimate goal is a "fruitful" organization, so that the ends of the earth will be reached with the gospel. To have a "fruitful" ministry may sound good, but this terminology is often just polite Christian language that really means "success" at virtually any cost.

The emerging generation of leaders like Mike and Patricia are wondering—both silently and out loud—whether they want to work with many of today's Christian leaders at all. If they do decide to participate, they often insist on contributing toward an altogether different kind of ministry culture. Describing these younger evangelicals, George Barna says "the means now justify the end,"[2] implying that the dysfunctional approaches of the past must yield to a deep desire for authenticity, integrity, and a prioritization not just on *what* we do, but on *how* we do it. This desire is more than a ministry mantra; it must be seen and felt to be real. If this does not happen, the unquenched thirst for authenticity becomes just one more dynamic in the alienation of people from our churches and Christian ministries.

MOTIVATION

On May 8th, 1993, the late Chris Farley debuted an unforgettable comedy routine on *Saturday Night Live*. The sketch depicted a family with two delinquent teenagers. Dad hires a speaker, "Matt Foley," to motivate his kids into better behavior. In addition to his disheveled and overweight appearance, Matt shouts insults at the teenagers, frequently loses his temper, and wallows in self-pity. Foley's trademark line is warning the teenagers that they could end up like himself, being "thirty-five years old, eating a steady diet of government cheese, and living in a van down by the river!" The routine concludes when his speech has impacted the teenagers, but only because they don't want to be like him.

Farley depicted this classic character many times. His hilarious shtick became one of the most popular in SNL's lineup; it's a depiction of all the motivational talks that do anything but motivate. Whether delivered by a zealous, manipulative manager or a slick marketer who has had too much coffee, most motivational efforts are intended to get people to do something that they really don't want to do. They are thinly veiled attempts to cajole people into delivering someone else's agenda. Our responses to these efforts are usually negative because they are symptomatic of a foundational flaw in leadership thinking.

In 2001, I was teaching a group of Christian executives on the topic of motivating people. We had gathered from various locations throughout Europe in the city of Vienna. I took my usual approach to present the material, explaining that leaders who adjust their behavior to the needs of those they lead—self-regulation—are better at motivating others. I demonstrated through research and several true stories that the outcome of this leadership behavior is a greater level of worker satisfaction, which in turn results in a higher level of productivity for the organization.

As I labored on, Branko, who had grown up under the Communist regime in Serbia, became visibly agitated. He knows well the Communist philosophy, tactics, and terminology of motivation. Finally, when he could no longer endure my presentation, he raised his hand and blurted out, "Your approach to Christian leadership is severely flawed. Your teaching implies that our ultimate motivation for practicing self-regulation is to get more productivity out of people so that the leaders and their organizations can be more successful."

"Yes, that's correct," I said. "Do you have a problem with that?"

"Yes," replied Branko. "I have a big problem with that. The leadership model you are proposing is virtually the same as the 'carrot and stick' approach that our Communist dictators have used for decades to oppress the masses."

Wow, what an indictment!

From my Western "if-it-works-it-must-be-right" orientation toward leadership, I could find nothing wrong with my teaching, but Branko methodically unraveled my arguments and helped me see that our ultimate motivation for leading changes everything. If my end game as a leader is to get more production out of those I lead, then I'll use self-regulation, praise, criticism, a hammer, or any other device that works. And what's more, I'll stop using the device if it doesn't produce the desired production in my followers.

Jesus' approach was radically different in that His ultimate motive for leading people was to help them reach their highest kingdom potential. His resolve to "build the church" was a high priority on Jesus' agenda, but progress toward that goal was always a by-product of this fundamental commitment to the development of His followers. This is revolutionary.

These days I still teach the benefits of self-regulation to leaders, but from a completely different perspective. Leaders are certainly accountable for results, and skills like self-regulation are helpful, but with one major twist: our primary role is to help those we lead be all that God wants them to be. That's radical, and it's risky. But as a Christ-centered leader, it's the right thing to do.

Since that encounter in Vienna, Branko and I have become good friends. Through him and others, I have been challenged to rethink and question many of my leadership assumptions. For starters, I asked myself the question, *How did our approach to Christian leadership develop this unhealthy intoxication with production and success in the first place?*

The Influence of Frederick Taylor's Theory

Frederick Winslow Taylor is generally regarded as the father of Scientific Management (also called Taylorism). Born in 1856 to a stern Quaker mother, young Frederick was brilliant and determined. In *Sequencing: Will Your Company be Innovative Over the Long Haul,* author Mike Metzger recounted how Taylor believed that sports ought to be played more efficiently, so he tinkered around with new groundstrokes in tennis and ended up winning the 1881 US national doubles tennis championship. He also developed new types of golf clubs, and became the handicap champion at the Philadelphia

Country Club in 1902, 1903, and 1905.[3] His determination and innovations paid off, but there was also a downside to his ideas.

When he turned to the workaday world in the 1880s and '90s, Taylor's principles of Scientific Management put a new twist on how work ought to be done. His theory was derived from Darwin's *Origin of the Species*. Like Darwin, Taylor believed that people are highly evolved animals, and his theory promoted the idea that people need to be "managed." The main framework of his scientific management fits neither Scripture nor human nature. For centuries it had been held that people are thinking, creative, responsible individuals. It was commonly understood that people manage assets, appetites, and animals, but not other people. Managing people is animalistic and dehumanizing, but the need for efficient people management was precisely Taylor's assessment of how work should be done.

In 1899, when the Bethlehem Steel Company asked him to use his theory to improve their worker efficiency, Taylor started with a question: *How many tons of pig-iron bars can a worker load onto a railcar in a working day?* He estimated the rate at which laborers loaded iron, and offered to double their wages if they worked harder. His solution was firing the less productive workers and hiring men with brute strength, whose intelligence he compared to that of an ox.[4] In other words, his theory regarded and treated people in the workplace as beasts. When profits didn't increase, Bethlehem Steel dismissed Taylor's theory.

But Taylor was undeterred; he continued to promote his ideas of scientific management. His principles might have been forgotten had he not met with a group of Harvard professors in the spring of 1908. Embracing his ideas, Harvard opened the first graduate school offering a master's degree in business later that year. It was based on the assumption that people ought to be "managed" by "experts." Taylor's ideas provided the cornerstone for twentieth century leadership. *Production is king. Efficiency is queen. And both come before people.*

The first assembly line workers easily recognized this. In *Shop Class as Soulcraft: An Inquiry into the Value of Work,* author

Matthew Crawford recalled how Henry Ford adopted Taylor's ideas and introduced the assembly line in 1913. Ford's new system prioritized efficiency, yielding the highest production to the detriment of people. But the assembly line provoked natural revulsion among the workers. It was so dehumanizing, in fact, that Ford's employees responded by walking off the job in droves. In order to keep 100 factory workers on the line, Ford had to hire 963 people! But before long the workers needed their jobs back so they became habituated over time to this de-evolutionary process. Thanks to the heuristic impact of Taylorism, assembly line employees eventually assumed the drabness and dullness of their work.[5]

To be fair, some historians cite evidence that Taylor had charitable intentions.[6] For example, he thought people could be trained to succeed. He also standardized tools and equipment to maximize human capability. What is now called ergonomics was an integral part of Taylorism. He was the first to fit people to jobs, both physically and psychologically, and to let facts and data do the talking rather than prejudice and opinions. He believed in giving feedback to employees, a central tenet in current participative management. He thought that labor strife was not inevitable—an extraordinary notion given the bitter, sometimes murderous, relations between employers and employees in his day. From these perspectives, Taylor, the man, seems to have had a genuine concern for people.

Regardless of Taylor's personal intentions, however, his Scientific Management had global implications on equal par with the teachings of Karl Marx. It influenced leaders as diverse as Vladimir Lenin and John D. Rockefeller, ultimately shaping both Communist and capitalist systems worldwide to view people as parts of the machinery to be exploited for optimal efficiency and effectiveness. Lenin, who ambivalently called Taylorism "a combination of the refined brutality of bourgeois exploitation and a number of the greatest scientific achievements," said, "We must organize in Russia the study of the Taylor system and systematically try it out and adapt it to our ends."[7]

Likewise, some major icons of Christian leadership who came of age in the last half of the twentieth century were deeply influenced by the principles of Taylorism; this paradigm prioritizes production and success, but tends to kick people to the curb. It may be disguised with nice motivational talk or dressed up in religious language, but it is still the foundation for most current leadership models that attempt to get people to work harder and produce more for the ultimate "success" of the leaders and the organization.

And what is the result of Taylor's approach to management among today's workforce? In his book *Coming Apart: The State of White America 1960-2010,* Charles Murray cites research that The General Social Survey has been conducting since 1973 among a large sampling of American workers.[8] Their study has intermittently asked white job interviewees to select one thing from a list they most preferred in a job. The workers are given the following choices:

- High income
- No danger of being fired
- Chances for advancement
- Short working hours
- A lot of free time
- Work that gives a feeling of accomplishment

For the first twenty years the survey was taken, results remained remarkably consistent. The first choice was always "work that gives a feeling of accomplishment." The two least-chosen first choices were always "short working hours" and "no danger of being fired." However, more recently the first choice of workers has radically shifted; "work that gives a feeling of accomplishment" has significantly declined while "short working hours" and "no danger of being fired" have doubled. Murray concludes that workers have become less interested in meaningful work and more interested in secure jobs with short working hours.

What caused this shift? Well, that may depend on your political perspective. One side of the political aisle tends to trace this trend to a dramatic collapse of industriousness in American culture. They cite statistics that show the U.S. has increasingly become an entitlement society, and people are less interested in meaningful work. The other side of the political aisle believes that these surveys reveal a workforce that has been overworked and abused by their employers, so current workers want less hours so they can pursue more desirable interests outside the workplace. Perhaps the answer is *both*.

Whatever the cause, the declining work ethic is due in no small part to employers and organizations that have attempted to squeeze every morsel of profit at the expense of their associates. Many Christian leaders have unfortunately conformed to similar patterns of thinking and behavior. For example, a worship pastor recently talked about the requirements placed upon him by his church leaders to direct multiple worship services each week. This gifted younger man is committed to ministry, but he is not sure he can continue to serve in a vocational church role. In another church, the lead pastor informed his staff that they should consider Sunday as their only day off. When the concerned youth pastor asked, "Who will do the ministry on Sunday morning?" he was told that he could find another job. Yet another younger leader recently stated that he resigned from a Christian ministry because their only interest was how many times he had presented their gospel tract in any given month. These individuals are committed to ministry, but they have serious questions about the motives behind the expectations placed upon them by institutional ministry leaders.

In *You Lost Me: Why Young Christians are Leaving Church . . . and Rethinking*, David Kinnaman describes the dropout problem inside the church. Kinnaman categorizes a large portion of these dropouts as "exiles" who are still invested in their faith but are stuck. Many people between the ages of 18 and 29 feel exiled from the church because their church isn't addressing the real questions of life. At the same time, they also feel exiled at work because their values are routinely dismissed. They are stuck between their culture and their church.

These young people have been raised in churches that evaluate success based primarily on numbers. Their pastors have focused their energy on getting money in the plate and keeping members in the pew. Religious activity, observe these exiles, is more about being productive rather than about being passionate for the Kingdom potential of people. They describe their churches as having slick programs and full sanctuaries in an effort to be impressive, but the leaders are mute and generally unhelpful when faced with real-world issues. When their parents' marriages crash or problems occur within their communities, the most these exiles can expect from their leaders are prayers and platitudes. For this reason, they have stopped looking to the church as a place to invest their passions, to pursue authentic relationships, or to develop their God-given gifts and abilities.[9]

The Impact of World War II on Ministry Leaders

Within a few years after the Second World War, a plethora of evangelical denominations, missions, and agencies based in North America sprouted into prominence by capitalizing on the triumphalism of the post-war era. For example, Billy Graham's 1949 evangelistic meetings in Los Angeles catapulted his ministry into the public eye. The Billy Graham Evangelistic Association made the strategic decision to capitalize on a military metaphor by referring to their rallies as "crusades" in which many thousands heard the gospel. Similarly, Bill Bright's Campus *Crusade* for Christ and Dick Hillis's Overseas *Crusades* were both launched in 1951, borrowing language from victorious Allies to imply that followers of Christ are called to rise up and win the world to Jesus.

It is understandable that ministries started in the generation following the Second World War had in mind an image of victory in warfare. Combined with Taylor's focus on productivity, this victory mindset was broadly embraced. It went on to spawn initiatives that emphasized global evangelization, including the Church Growth Movement, A.D. 2000, World by Radio, and Saturation Church Planting, to name just a few. As a result, the second half of the twentieth century will be remembered in history as a period of great advance for Christian faith worldwide.

We owe a great debt of gratitude to these movements and their outstanding leaders. There is something attractive about the notion of spiritual battle with the attendant thought, "If we're going to win the world for Christ, then we must be a large and strong organization." But this crusading spirit provided the nesting ground for prioritizing success. Bigger churches and bigger missions became the focus. Books and recordings and seminars abounded that taught the secrets to becoming successful. Seminaries filled classes with disciples of the "church growth movement." These courses and resources were consumed in the West and then exported to every continent as the "Christian" model for organizations. The triumphal zeal that came out of the Allied victory morphed into a flawed model that applauds success for our personal kingdoms in the name of "fruitfulness."

Again, this is not to suggest that a large ministry is inherently wrong. Progress and productivity can be good things. But our rampant emphasis on growth measured by comparative numbers becomes a dilemma that misses dynamics like courage, faithfulness in the face of opposition, and the prophetic voice as essential marks of Christian effectiveness. As the slogan "bigger is better" has covertly dominated evangelical attitudes and agendas, leaders have inevitably adopted patterns of thinking and behavior that are in conflict with their core calling.

No doubt most Christian leaders never mean for it to turn out this way. They start out in their leadership roles with strong convictions and honorable intentions. But as they have opportunity to advance, they face subtle yet important decisions. In those moments, it is easy to assume that the goal above all others is to reach as many people as possible. Over time the priority of success trumps all else. It eventually becomes the air they breathe.

I recently ran headlong into my own tendencies, even though I should know better. During a visit to Asia to conduct a leadership seminar, I was the honored guest, the public speaker, the expert. I was separated from the other participants and given the best room, with personal service. I made all the appropriate comments about how unsettled I felt to be placed in such a privileged position, but to be honest, part of me wanted it. It somehow fed in me that longing to stand out from the crowd.

None of us is above these temptations. It's like criticizing people with expensive vehicles. Years ago, a popular question was: "Would Jesus drive a BMW?" The expected answer was, of course, "No, Jesus would not drive a BMW. Therefore, good Christians should not drive a BMW." I'm not sure why BMW owners became the focus of criticism rather than people who owned a Lexus or Porsche. In any case, the arguments for that statement may appear to be sound, and I can spout that message—until I get to have a Bimmer myself. The temptation is to give all kinds of reasons why my circumstances are unique, but these examples demonstrate that power and status are intoxicating and behave like a magnet by pulling well-intentioned leaders away from their original principles. As Charles Colson famously said, "It's difficult to stand on a pedestal and wash the feet of those below."

THE LOOK OF LEADERSHIP TODAY

According to the dictionary, the word *tradition* comes from the Latin *traditio*, meaning "to hand down" or "to hand over." The word is used in a number of ways in the English language, but it generally refers to a custom or set of customs taught by one generation to another. A tradition establishes the norm over time; in other words, it determines how something should be done. The time needed to establish a tradition can be quite short. In Christian leadership today, it is only three or four generations, less than seventy-five years.

Top-down Leadership: Theory X

If traditions for today's Christian leaders are based on Taylor's Scientific Management and global domination that originated in military triumph, then we can see that norms for today's Christian leaders are more about having power and being successful than about helping people reach their potential. Therefore, the traditional form of Christian leadership today is characterized by status, power, and control. We may choose different words in our effort to spiritualize this reality, but the leader's need for status, power, and control has become the reigning order.

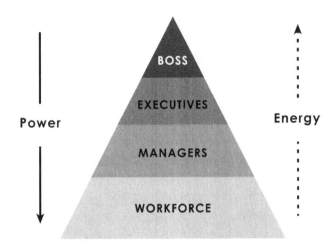

The graphic above shows a traditional hierarchical structure within organizations; this leadership motif is the "top-down" model. At the top of the triangle is the senior leader (boss). Just below the boss are several levels of leadership. Different ministry organizations have varying levels, but the bottom level is typically populated by the workforce. The solid arrow on the left running from top to bottom shows the downward flow of power. The higher up on the pyramid one moves, the greater his or her level of authority and power in the organization. The broken arrow on the right running from bottom to top demonstrates the flow of energy. In this traditional structure, the primary energy from the workforce is expended to satisfy the desires and goals of the boss and senior leaders.

This model is ingrained in Western Christian organizations and has frequently been a major export from the West to other parts of the world. So deeply ingrained is it in most ministry organizations, in fact, that only recently have people begun to question its validity.

The following issues have been identified as some of the weaknesses of the top-down model.

First, the model implies that "vision" is the exclusive domain of the leaders on top of the pyramid. It is generally perceived that those who populate the upper tiers of the pyramid have reached their position on the basis of their greater wisdom and spirituality. These leaders don't sit down one day and consciously think, "I am wiser and more spiritual; therefore, I should climb higher." (Perhaps some do, but most do not.) Rather, this thinking often originates at a *subconscious* level. And when they receive a promotion, the leaders face the pressure of needing to appear and sound wiser or more spiritual than they know themselves to be. Many begin to live a façade, keeping up appearances to meet the expectations of others. They begin to isolate themselves, resisting the accountability and feedback they so desperately need.

Second, the top-down model also underlines the dynamic of rank or status. It works with the perceptions of "more than" and "less than." This model is usually embedded by the organization's reward system that highlights status. In a hierarchical structure, it is not hard to know one's place. One is not unaware of the difficulty of moving to a higher level on the pyramid, since status is so fiercely guarded by those who possess it. This is particularly relevant in those parts of the world where the mindset "you are what you do" is entrenched in the culture. This, too, is antithetical to Christ-centered principles.

Third, the top-down leadership model emphasizes the importance of power and authority, the key elements of a status mentality. In this view, the more power a person has the more important and successful he or she feels. Power is intoxicating, so it is held tightly, regardless of the person's actual ability to lead. In many instances, this results in the blocking of wisdom and skill from others in the organization who do not have sufficient status to warrant a hearing from those with power and authority. This often means that ministries fail to reap the benefits of all their people. It's like hiring a brain surgeon and then making her fix bandages for people with minor injuries.

The top-down model is fueled by a set of assumptions that leaders have toward followers. The MIT management professor Douglas McGregor, a contemporary of Abraham Maslow, examined theories on the behavior of individuals at work and, based on his observations, identified various assumptions that leaders possess toward their coworkers. In his 1960 book, *The Human Side of Enterprise*, McGregor used the term "Theory X" to describe the assumptions leaders have of themselves and the people they lead in the traditional, top-down organizational structure.[10]

"Theory X" Leadership Assumptions

- The average person dislikes work and will avoid it if possible.
- People lack motivation, innovation, and are not goal-oriented; therefore, control and threats must be used to pressure them into action.
- The average person prefers to be directed and dislikes taking responsibility.
- Tough management is required if an organization wants to reach its goals; therefore, firmness and micro-management are frequently necessary.
- The average person needs direction more than development.
- People depend on the intelligence of their leaders.

Predictably, these "Theory X" assumptions easily translate into an "us and them" mentality between the boss and the workers. Not all of these assumptions are held by everyone subscribing to a traditional model of leadership, of course, but the assumptions are prevalent. It might require some soul-searching for a leader to recognize that some of these elements exist in his or her own attitudes toward people, since they come so naturally in today's traditional leadership culture.

Participative Leadership: Theory Y

It would be altogether discouraging if we were to shut McGregor's book at this point and resign ourselves to live in the arena of a top-down power, status, and control type of leadership. But there is hope.

What Douglas McGregor also found in his research is that other leaders have a very different set of assumptions. They have not bought into the "traditional leadership model" coming from Scientific Management theory. Instead, these leaders assume that people are thinking, creative, responsible individuals of value, and McGregor refers to them as "Theory Y" leaders. They typically have the following assumptions about others with whom they work.

"Theory Y" Leadership Assumptions

- People view work as a natural part of their lives.
- The average person is internally motivated to reach objectives to which he or she is committed.
- People will pursue common goals when they are properly encouraged.
- They will seek and accept responsibility under favorable conditions.
- People have the capacity to be innovative in solving problems.
- People are independently intelligent and will excel when trusted to do so.

Additionally, McGregor's research observed that both "Theory X" and "Theory Y" leadership assumptions contain a self-fulfilling prophecy. In other words, people tend to behave consistently with the assumptions that leaders have of them. The way leaders view their people predicts how they will treat those people. If a leader views and treats them as intelligent and motivated, then the people will generally respond with more intelligent and motivated behavior. If, on the contrary, the leader views and treats the people as irresponsible, then they will display a more passive, dependent work style.

COMMUNICATING "THEORY X" AND "THEORY Y" WITH STORYCENTRIC LEARNERS

The sections above propose that top-down leadership behavior usually stems from a leader's "Theory X" way of viewing their followers. The development of healthy leadership behavior must therefore begin with a "Theory Y" way of viewing followers. This applies to leaders everywhere.

So how can storycentric learners more easily grasp the impact of McGregor's "Theory X" and "Theory Y" ways of viewing followers? The exercise below uses the tools of storycentric communication including a fictional story, discussion questions, and images to teach how a leader's view of himself and others can deeply affect his or her legacy.

Story: The Shadow of a Leader[11]

The celebration had been organized to recognize Dr. Benyam and his twenty years of successful ministry. In addition, he was to be ordained the new general director of the Grace of God denomination. The crowd listened carefully as the program began, and everyone rose to their feet when Dr. Benyam was proclaimed general director. The charge was given that all should awaken from their sleep and make the Grace of God denomination the shadow of a great leader!

No one in the audience would disagree with the impact of Dr. Benyam's ministry. But one person was overheard to say, "If Fishers of Men Ministry is his shadow, then the Grace of God denomination is in trouble."

Dr. Benyam deserved praise for many reasons. He had grown up with a father who offered little praise but much punishment, and his childhood was one of loneliness and rejection. When he became an adult, he was driven by a deep inward desire to make a difference. Benyam was a gifted Christian leader in his youth, a consistent voice for integrity and change in the church and in his community. He founded the Fishers of Men Ministry (FMM) to equip Christian believers to reach their own people.

Few would say that "Brother Benyam," as everyone called him years before, was the same person who now stood on the platform. As they left the celebration, Samuel and Sarah, the only two members of the original Fishers of Men Ministry (FMM) team, discussed how Brother Benyam and FMM had changed.

The first years of FMM were exciting. Brother Benyam was a team player and inspired others with his vision and encouragement. Churches welcomed FMM's evangelism training, which proved ideal for those who were eager to reach their friends for Christ. But as time passed, Benyam's leadership approach began to change. Although it didn't happen overnight, the close friendships he'd had with the FMM team, particularly with Samuel and Sarah, steadily grew more distant.

As FMM grew under Benyam's leadership, he was invited to travel and teach and, in the process, became a sought-after conference speaker. It wasn't long before the early signs of "big boss sickness" began to appear. At first, no one seemed to notice. There was no objection when Benyam moved into a large office. After all, this is common among church leaders, as is the privilege of a car and driver. As they reflected on this, Samuel and Sarah could not help remarking that Benyam had previously lived a humble and simple life.

As pressure on his time increased, the spontaneous prayer meetings gave way to weekly chapel sessions always led by the Director, who was always addressed as "Dr." He began to spend little time with the FMM team, and a policy was even put in place restricting access to him! The difficulty of seeing Dr. Benyam without scheduling an appointment should have been a danger sign, but no one seemed to think it strange.

As Samuel and Sarah discussed the past, they realized how Dr. Benyam had eventually taken control of every aspect of the ministry. He insisted on making every ministry decision and approving every financial expenditure, which resulted in numerous delays and lost ministry opportunities.

Instead of encouraging new ideas and initiatives, Dr. Benyam no longer tolerated deviation from his directives. Those offering a differing opinion suffered in various ways, ranging from being shamed to being fired from their position. Morale began to deteriorate in every department. Promising younger workers left as quickly as possible to find a ministry position that offered more acceptance and support.

As they analyzed the course of events, Samuel and Sarah were forced to conclude that Dr. Benyam had fallen guilty to misusing the power of his office. It had become a means for self-fulfillment and advancement instead of service. They ruefully realized that their original sense of community with their friend and brother was probably lost forever.

Questions for Discussion

- How would you describe Benyam's early leadership?
- How would you describe Benyam's later leadership?
- What are some possible explanations for the change in Benyam's leadership?

In addition to the use of story, the pertinent points of "The Shadow of a Leader" can be communicated with images and song. As the image above shows, the "big man" leader casts a small shadow and has little lasting influence while the humble leader casts a much bigger shadow with greater influence. A song has been produced in several Asian and African languages to contrast good and poor leadership outcomes. The final verse encourages leaders to seek wisdom from God, trust the good people around them, and bring blessings to those they lead.

"Theory Y" Leader Stories

Those who see their coworkers through "Theory Y" eyes are the bright spots of hope in today's crop of Christian leaders. They demonstrate respect and give opportunity for others to give valuable input. Liz Wiseman calls these leaders "multipliers."[12] Everyone around them seems to get smarter and more capable, because they invoke each person's unique abilities and encourage collective intelligence.

My friend Jane is one such multiplier. I was once invited to attend a staff meeting of the organization that she leads. During those two hours, several people shared responsibility to lead various aspects of the meeting. Although Jane is very capable and highly respected in her field of expertise, she was notably low-profile in the meeting. She demonstrated her commitment to develop staff members by engaging them with provocative questions. She wasn't the center of attention and didn't seem to worry about how smart she looked. She spoke only about 10 percent of the time, mostly just to ask questions or polish a problem statement, and then backed away to give the team space to find an answer. I quizzed Jane on her approach to leadership after the meeting.

"Often the team's ideas actually turn out to be much better than I could ever generate on my own," she quickly responded.

As I spoke to those who work with Jane, one of them commented: "She makes me feel like I'm valuable, and she gets my very best."

We need more leaders like Jane. So how can leaders and their ministries change? Is it even possible?

For many years, Walt was a "top-down" ministry leader. He was known for getting things done, even at the expense of good people. He was focused on results and was tough on those under his supervision. He ran his ministry division with an iron hand and took pride in his ability to generate fear among his coworkers. He maintained tight control of nearly every ministry activity. When staff turnover was high, Walt absolved himself by saying that the call to ministry required high levels of sacrifice and few were willing to make it. He refused to admit that the turnover rate might have anything to with his leadership style. He believed his primary leadership task was to motivate the unmotivated, or at least to make sure people were not slacking in their jobs.

But then something changed within Walt. It didn't happen all at once, but slowly God began to open his eyes to envision another way to lead. First, he recognized that his need to control was generated by his own fear of failure. He saw that God alone can turn people's hearts from fear to confidence in His sufficiency. This turned Walt into a man of sincere prayer. Second, he acknowledged that God has called leaders to faithfulness. God alone is responsible for the increase; we are only responsible to plant and nurture the seed. Third, he began to recognize the potential of others and slowly started to trust them.

Today Walt is a completely different leader. He is appreciative, affirming, and great to be around. Most importantly, he is having an enormous, lasting influence on those around him. And the work of the ministry is getting done. It is healthy, growing, and biblically fruitful.

Jane's and Walt's stories describe leaders who view their followers through McGregor's "Theory Y" construct.

What Do You See, a Water Pump or a Rice Field?

Here's another example of teaching "Theory X" and "Theory Y" to storycentric learners.

Typically, most leaders "see" the church and the people they lead in one of two ways: as a water pump or as a rice field.

The Water Pump Way

Sample Discovery Questions:

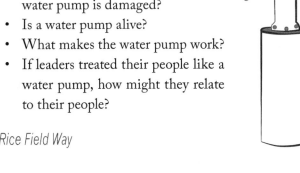

- What is the purpose of a water pump?
- What are the parts of a water pump?
- What happens when a part of the water pump is damaged?
- Is a water pump alive?
- What makes the water pump work?
- If leaders treated their people like a water pump, how might they relate to their people?

The Rice Field Way

Sample Discovery Questions:

- What is the purpose of a rice field?
- What are the parts of a rice field?
- What happens when a plant in the rice field is damaged?
- Is a rice field alive?
- What makes the rice field work?

- If leaders treated their people like a rice field, how might they relate to their people?

Four key principles of effective storycentric communication are reflected in the exercise above. First, the image is used as a focal point to assist learners to enter into dialogue about how they "see" the people they lead. With an image in mind, the discussion flows more easily. Second, the repetitiveness of the questions between the two images aids recall. Third, keeping the discovery questions related to the image actually enhances the application and potential of positive change in leadership style. And fourth, vivid images of a water pump or a rice field will perpetually come to mind whenever the storycentric learner encounters a leader who demonstrates these tendencies.

Relating these images to Paul's words in 1 Corinthians 3:4–9 adds all the more to the power of storycentric learning:

> [4] For when one says, "I follow Paul," and another, "I follow Apollos," are you not being merely human? [5] What then is Apollos? What is Paul? Servants through whom you believed, as the Lord assigned to each. [6] I planted, Apollos watered, but God gave the growth. [7] So neither he who plants nor he who waters is anything, but only God who gives the growth. [8] He who plants and he who waters are one, and each will receive his wages according to his labor. [9] For we are God's fellow workers. You are God's field, God's building.

Related Discovery Question

- According to these verses and our discussions, do you think Paul the apostle sees the church and the people he leads more like a water pump or more like a rice field?

Without telling listeners what they "must, ought, or should" remember, storycentric learners come to acknowledge that a "water pump" leader tends to (1) use people, (2) control people, and (3) try to control production. On the other hand, a "rice field" leader tends to (1) cultivate people, (2) release people, and (3) allows God to control production. This communication approach has tended to elicit a deep desire within the storycentric learner to avoid being a "water pump" leader like Dr. Benyam and instead to choose to become a "rice field" leader like Jane and Walt.

Is it even possible to change the way we lead? Yes, it is! We don't have to settle with our current state. Despite the fact that fallen human nature has affected all leaders in every culture, God can transform leaders. To borrow a word from church history, we need a "reformation" in our understanding and practice of leadership. Like the Christians of centuries past, returning to the wisdom of God is our wellspring for a hopeful future, and the Spirit of God will enable us to follow the greatest leadership example of all time: Jesus Christ.

CHAPTER 7 SUMMARY

- Although examples of Christ-centered leaders dot the landscape of Christian ministry, the credibility of many current Christian leaders is sadly compromised.
- Ministry leaders often prioritize their own success and the organization's success at the expense of their own integrity and the welfare of others.
- The current quest for success has historical roots in Frederick Winslow Taylor's Scientific Management theory. This theory dominated the field of management science for much of the twentieth century, and has indelibly shaped many current ministry contexts where people are used to achieve the leaders' agenda and organizational productivity.
- Douglas MacGregor's Theory X and Theory Y are explained in light of the current ministry leadership climate. Examples of teaching these theories to storycentric learners are provided.

LEADERSHIP REFORMATION

The current state of Christian leadership is in disrepair. The quest for success has overshadowed the Christ-centered attributes of faithfulness, integrity, and service. Productivity is placed above people. Many under our charge feel like exiles as their passion for the Lord is not finding expression in the church. But we don't have to settle with today's "traditional" model of Christian leadership. A reformation *can* occur that will return us to the teaching and leadership example of Jesus Christ.

A LEGITIMATE LEADERSHIP MODEL

Before we consider Him as our leadership model, it is appropriate to explore the question: Is the life and leadership of Jesus Christ a legitimate example to follow? After all, Jesus was the unique Son of God and has the distinction of being unlike any person who ever lived. Since He is "one of a kind," does that place Him in a category immeasurably beyond us? Is a leadership model derived from the King of kings and Lord of lords, who possessed the full arsenal of heaven, even relevant for us?

Various biblical images provide bridges for interpreting Jesus' life and ministry as a relevant model for us today. First, the Scriptures portray Him as fully divine but also fully human: "Since therefore the children share in flesh and blood, [Jesus] himself likewise partook of the same things" (Heb 2:14). Jesus was genuinely and completely human. He fully experienced our mortality, and He functioned within the legitimate confines and potential of His own humanity.

The writer of Hebrews goes on to sum up Jesus' example this way: "For we do not have a high priest who is unable to sympathize with our weaknesses, but one who in every respect has been tempted as we are, yet without sin" (Heb 4:15). By this we know that Jesus faced the same temptations that all leaders face. The way He prevailed amidst the adverse challenges of leadership in His day gives us an example to follow in ours.

Second, Jesus' leadership was both culturally relevant for His time and transculturally applicable for all time. He was born Jewish and grew up under Roman occupation in Palestine, and His culture was, in fact, very similar to the storycentric communities in our day. Additionally, as a member of a certain clan, Jesus was fully recognized as one of their own. His identification with this family and society was so complete that when He began His public ministry, the crowds in His hometown asked, "Is not this the carpenter's son?" (Matt 13:55). They clearly regarded Him as a local boy.

There was nothing outwardly abstract about Jesus' life. Like everyone else, He was surrounded with real people in real circumstances, and He demonstrated effective ministry in that particular context. The principles by which Jesus led were completely authentic in His specific time and place; but down through the centuries these principles have been applied in diverse contexts all across the globe and found to be just as effective, relevant, and appropriate.

Jesus Institutes a New Leadership in the New Covenant

"Do not think that I have come to abolish the Law or the Prophets," Jesus said in the Sermon on the Mount. "I have not come to abolish them but to fulfill them" (Matt 5:17). He then proceeded to teach a whole new way of relating to God. His death and physical resurrection fulfilled the Old Covenant and introduced the beginning of the promised New Covenant between God and His people. The curtain has been torn in two, and a new order has been ushered in. These events have cataclysmic implications both for God's people and for Christian leaders today.

Paul the apostle explains the difference Jesus' followers make as ministers of the New Covenant. Because of God's unmerited grace, we now have life, righteousness, and freedom in a way not known before. Paul's explanation in 2 Corinthians 3 highlights the contrast between the two covenants.

Old Covenant	New Covenant
The Old Covenant was written on tablets of stone with ink.	The New Covenant is written on tablets of human hearts with the Spirit (v. 3).
The Old Covenant was of the letter that kills.	The New Covenant is of the Spirit that gives life (v. 6).
The Old Covenant was a ministry of condemnation.	The New Covenant is a ministry of righteousness (v. 9).
The Old Covenant no longer has glory.	The New Covenant's surpassing glory is permanent (v. 10).
The Old Covenant was a veiled ministry.	The New Covenant is unveiled and is a ministry of freedom (vv. 16–17).

When we compare these two covenants side by side, we cannot ignore the implications. The New Covenant is radically different from the Old and it calls for a new kind of leadership. Although we can glean helpful lessons from the examples of Moses, Joshua, Nehemiah, and David, all of whom were leaders during the Old Covenant era, we are now liberated to operate under the New Covenant in which Jesus is our supreme and primary leadership model.

In His post-resurrection appearance to the disciples in Jerusalem, Jesus said, "You will receive power when the Holy Spirit has come upon you" (Acts 1:8). The coming of the Spirit at Pentecost confirmed the New Covenant paradigm of Christian leadership. Prior to this, the Holy Spirit would only come upon and anoint special people at special times for special purposes—to be a king or a prophet, for example (Ex 29:7; 2 Kgs 9:6). In addition to anointing some others for artistic endeavors (Ex 31:1–5) and the anointing of the tabernacle (Ex 40:9), the notion of anointing was reserved to signify God's elite blessing and empowerment on His "chosen ones." It was reserved for called-out leaders and signaled a special status.

When we turn the page from the Old Testament to the Gospels, we find the anointing of God reserved exclusively for the Messiah to spread the good news of the kingdom of God and to set free those who have been held captive (Luke 4:18–19; Acts 10:38). Finally, on the Day of Pentecost, the Spirit was given to all believers (John 14:16; Rom 8:9). As the epistles tell us, *all* Christians are now anointed and chosen for the purpose of advancing God's kingdom (2 Cor 1:21–22; 1 John 2:20, 27). After Jesus, the only instructions for anointing specific individuals was for elders in praying for the sick (Jas 5:14–15).

In other words, after Pentecost the term "anointed" is applied only to the collective body of believers in a general sense. The New Testament writers never refer to any elite category of anointed leaders. Rather, we all are anointed by God with the Holy Spirit to do the "greater works" that Jesus had predicted (John 14:12).

What difference does this make to leadership in the body of Christ? It actually makes a lot of difference. Any reference to a leader having a special "anointing" is to impose an inappropriate status not endorsed by Jesus. The label tends to create undue separation between leaders and followers, which is not consistent with New Testament teaching. Every believer is anointed with the Spirit of God, and Jesus desires each of us to serve in our diverse giftedness with Him as our anointed Head. We follow the One who introduced a New Covenant model of leadership, operating through the ministry of the Spirit who gives life and freedom and grace.

Jesus Establishes a New Leadership Symbol with a Towel

John 13:3–14 is one biblical account that provides a powerful image of Jesus' leadership perspectives and practice:

> Jesus, knowing that the Father had given all things into his hands, and that he had come from God and was going back to God, rose from supper. He laid aside his outer garments, and taking a towel, tied it around his waist. Then he poured water into a basin and began to wash the disciples' feet and to wipe them with the towel that was wrapped around him.
>
> He came to Simon Peter, who said to him, "Lord, do you wash my feet?"
>
> Jesus answered him, "What I am doing you do not understand now, but afterward you will understand."
>
> Peter said to him, "You shall never wash my feet."
>
> Jesus answered him, "If I do not wash you, you have no share with me."
>
> Simon Peter said to him, "Lord, not my feet only but also my hands and my head!"
>
> Jesus said to him, "The one who has bathed does not need to wash, except for his feet, but is completely clean. And you are clean, but not every one of you." For he knew who was to betray him; that was why he said, "Not all of you are clean."
>
> When he had washed their feet and put on his outer garments and resumed his place, he said to them, "Do you understand what I have done to you? You call me Teacher and Lord, and you are right, for so I am. If I then, your Lord and Teacher, have washed your feet, you also ought to wash one another's feet."

The time was Passover, the most sacred of Jewish feasts. Three million pilgrims would have been in Jerusalem for the Celebration Week. Word had spread like wildfire that Jesus of Nazareth was on His way to the feast. Thousands lined the road as Jesus entered the city, waving palm branches and chanting, "Hosanna! Blessed is he who comes in the name of the Lord. Blessed is the kingdom of our father David!"

But Jesus wasn't what the crowd expected. They were looking for a conquering king, and He would disappoint them that same week by dying on a cross. But in defying their expectations, He fulfilled their most profound need. This is made explicitly clear a few days later, when Jesus washed the feet of His disciples after the Passover meal.

Remember that the roads of first-century Palestine were not paved or tarred but plain dirt. In dry weather they were deep in dust, and in wet weather they could become slippery mud. People did not wear shoes in those days; they wore simple sandals consisting of a flat sole held onto the feet by a few straps. A walk in the street inevitably soiled the feet, which is why a basin of water and a towel sat just inside the doorway of homes. The custom was for a servant to greet visitors and wash their feet as they entered.

But on this night when Jesus gathered His disciples for a meal, the washbasin was sitting unused. The disciples' thoughts were occupied with more noble things than dusty feet. The talk of the week had ignited their imaginations of the kingdom of God, and they were dreaming of thrones and power and glory—so much so that they even squabbled about which of them would be the greatest in this kingdom! Only one person noticed that everybody in the house had dirty feet.

Jesus got up from the table, prepared Himself, and started to wash His disciples' feet. Here is the King of kings, washing people's feet and drying them with a towel. Here is a King whose symbol of authority is a towel.

As we teach this pivotal text on Christ-centered leadership in storycentric settings, we recite the story as John told it. We often use a simple towel as an image to represent the story. Then we ask the following series of questions:

1. What is happening in this story?
2. How did Jesus influence His followers in this story—through positional power or by serving them?
3. Based on His example, whose feet did Jesus want His disciples to wash?

These questions facilitate participants to discover through exploration the following leadership principles from this story.

Jesus' Use of the "Towel" Represents His Whole Life and Leadership

The image of the towel dramatizes not only Jesus' leadership style, but also His whole life. Washing the disciples' feet was no isolated incident. On the contrary, what Jesus did that night in the upper room vividly portrays the entire journey He made from the Father into the world and back to the Father. Jesus laid aside His garments as He had laid aside His glory in heaven. He gave up His privileges as the group's leader as He had given up His privileges as the Son of God. He performed a menial act of service to foreshadow the degrading death He would endure the next day. And when He had finished the task of washing their feet, Jesus once again took up His garments and returned to His place of honor at the table, just as He was taken up from the grave and seated once more with God the Father.

In the upper room, the Son of Man stripped off His garments, got down on His knees, and washed the dirt off the feet of those whom He had called to follow Him. This final act of service before Calvary was a fitting symbol of His whole life and leadership.

Jesus' Use of the "Towel" Reveals His Perspective on Positional Power

Jesus' use of the towel also revealed His concept of positional power. From a human perspective, washing feet is beneath the dignity of a king. Peter, shocked at Jesus' actions, vehemently declared, "You shall never wash my feet!" Apart from recognizing his own unworthiness, Peter also wanted Jesus to fit into earthly ideas of royalty and privilege.

With this act, Jesus dismantled the human concepts of position and pecking order. We live with the notion that to be a leader is to be exalted, but in His use of the towel, Jesus revealed that being God means coming down from His throne and giving Himself to serve.

Jesus' Use of the "Towel" Teaches Us to Serve God by Serving Others

"Do you understand what I have done to you?" Jesus asked His disciples after washing their feet. "You call me Teacher and Lord, and you are right, for so I am. If I then, your Lord and Teacher, have washed your feet, you also ought to wash one another's feet."

Peter and the rest would have been perfectly comfortable washing Jesus' feet, for it would have been normal according to human ideas. But what Jesus did went against the grain of everything they had ever known about leadership. It was diametrically opposite to what they expected of a leader. And then Jesus added, "If I then . . . have washed your feet, you also ought to wash one another's feet."

Jesus' words imply that we serve God by serving others. Our neighbor is our duty and responsibility, and we serve Jesus when we serve them. Reflecting on Jesus' instructions, Darrell Johnson said that we wash our Lord's feet as we "wash the feet" of others. Our spouses and children and friends are the ones to receive our service and sacrifice. We honor God when we honor them. Our ministry colleagues are the ones to receive our attention and assistance. We build His kingdom when we build them up.[1]

When a leader follows Jesus' example, their resume will no longer say, "I don't wash feet." Washing feet is *precisely* what a leader does, because it's what Jesus did.

Jesus never used the word "leader" to describe the Twelve. Although He spent the majority of His ministry years investing in those who would lead the church, the values of the day were not what He wanted to transfer to His disciples. The conventional leadership values of Jesus' day projected an image that is not very different from our times. Leaders were proud, oppressive, and promoted themselves into seats of positional authority. Jesus was unafraid to point out the defects of the teachers and Pharisees, even going so far as to call them "hypocrites," "white-washed sepulchers," and "snakes."

Like the religious leaders of Jesus' day, much of what ministry leaders today believe and do in the realm of power and control has been borrowed, not from the Scriptures, but from surrounding secular institutions. Just as the teachers and Pharisees seated themselves in the chair of Moses (Matt 23:1), we have confused positional power and spiritual leadership. By blending the two, we have made them appear as one and the same, only to produce a toxic concoction that has destroyed many. To save us from just such a scenario, Jesus demonstrated and advocated metaphors such as "servant," "steward," and "shepherd," metaphors that formed alternative mental models for leadership as the early church was established.

Just before riding into Jerusalem that final week, Jesus told His disciples, "For even the Son of Man came not to be served but to serve, and to give his life as a ransom for many" (Mark 10:45). With this one line He turned everything upside down.

If we are to lead as Jesus led, there will be no room for seeking power and control. Nor will there be any place for competition and jockeying for position. We will have no reason to compare ourselves or our "success" with that of others on the rungs of the leadership ladder. A Lord who comes to meet my deepest needs with a towel in His hands changes everything. "A God on his knees before me humbles me and strangely makes me more God-centered. You see, if my only view of God is that of a supreme king at the summit of the chain of command, a king on the top rung of the ladder, it makes me much more self-centered. I'm always wondering how I will get to him and worrying about how I am doing: *Am I making progress toward him? What can I do to make my way up to him?* In the name of religion, we become preoccupied with ourselves. Not so when God is kneeling before us in self-emptying love. We cannot help but be preoccupied with him. Such love knocks us off our throne and out of our centers. He becomes the center."[2] In so doing, Jesus was revealing the King's own idea about what it means to be King.

This way of relating to people as a leader isn't normal. It is subversive. It reverses the conventional order. It destabilizes. But this is what Jesus intended. The gospel of the kingdom changes our whole concept of power, of authority, and of status. When the disciples were arguing about who would be greatest, Jesus said to them,

> "You know that the rulers of the Gentiles lord it over them, and their great ones exercise authority over them. It shall not be so among you. But whoever would be great among you must be your servant, and whoever would be first among you must be your slave, even as the Son of Man came not to be served but to serve, and to give his life as a ransom for many." (Matt 20:25–28)

This King who led with a towel inaugurated a kingdom of foot washers committed to meeting the deepest needs of others. He deposed the icon of leaders clamoring for power, people clambering over each other to get to the top. Jesus' example even puts to rest the notion that I wash your feet so that you will wash mine. Or, to put it in modern lingo, "I scratch your back, you scratch mine." Rather, I wash your feet so that you will in turn wash another's feet.

Jesus' use of the towel is extremely relevant today. The way He led in a specific culture at a particular time speaks to leadership in all cultures in every age of history. He turned the world on its head when He intentionally defied human expectations and chose instead to lead from His knees with a towel in hand. Thus, by creating a new image of what a leader is supposed to be, Jesus provided a model for us to follow.

The church today desperately needs a leadership reformation that goes back to what we know to be true and right. To state it more directly, we need Jesus as our leadership model.

CHAPTER 8 SUMMARY

- The leadership of Jesus Christ is presented as a model for today's ministry leaders. His model is legitimate for two reasons: (1) He was fully divine and fully human, so He faced temptation as all leaders do, and (2) His leadership was both culturally relevant for His time and transculturally applicable for all time.
- Jesus instituted a New Covenant that was intended to affect all ministry leadership.
- Jesus established a new leadership symbol with a towel. Jesus' use of the towel represented His whole life and leadership. His use of the towel revealed his perspective on positional power. And His use of the towel teaches ministry leaders to serve God by serving others.

9
LEADING WITH A LONG VIEW

In addition to the image of "leading with a towel" in the story-centric learner's mind, several significant characteristics of Jesus' life and ministry are especially relevant to leaders. These principles provide the basic building blocks for understanding and applying a leadership that is truly Christ-centered.

First of all, Jesus had a long-view perspective. Someone has said that the difference between leaders and followers is perspective, and the difference between good leaders and great leaders is better perspective. Jesus, the greatest of all leaders, had a crystal-clear perspective on His transcendent role for the future of the human race.

The Son of God was completely centered on doing the Father's will. He knew exactly who He was and what He had come to earth to do. As He Himself said, Jesus was fulfilling all that had preceded Him in Jewish history (Matt 5:17; Luke 4:16–19). Throughout His earthly ministry, this sense of purpose influenced Jesus' daily plans and activities (Mark 14:21; John 13:1). In one post-resurrection appearance, He explained to the disciples, "These are my words that I spoke to you while I was still with you, that everything written about me in the Law of Moses and the Prophets and the Psalms must be fulfilled" (Luke 24:44). Jesus' appreciation of history and vision of future redemption reflected His resolve to fulfill His divine purpose by faithfully accomplishing the Father's will (John 4:34; 6:39).

The Father's mission was to sacrifice His Son to save humankind and to reconcile all things to Himself. Jesus' revealed this mission when He declared, "For even the Son of Man came not to be served but to serve, and to give his life as a ransom for many" (Mark 10:45). And later the Apostle Paul explained, "For in [Christ] all the fullness of God was pleased to dwell, and through him to reconcile to himself all things, whether on earth or in heaven, making peace by the blood of his cross" (Col 1:19–20). Jesus' mission was therefore not a short-term focus on the three decades He spent on earth. Nor did He focus exclusively on the twelve men who would lead after His departure. His perspective was not even limited to the century immediately ahead. Jesus' long-view perspective was His unique role in the redemption of *the whole human race* and the reconciliation of *all creation* (Rom 8:20–23).

From start to finish, Jesus carried out His ministry with a steadfast focus on the final destination in mind. This long-term perspective, though tested and challenged, never wavered. Storycentric learners often resonate with the narrative where Satan tempted Jesus at the outset of His ministry with a pragmatic shortcut, a quick and easy means of reaching His goal. He took Jesus to a high mountain and showed Him all the kingdoms of the world in all their glory, and said, "All these I will give you." Storycentric leaders grapple with questions and dramas that facilitate them to embrace how Jesus resisted each of Satan's temptations (Matt 4:8–9).

On another occasion, when Jesus foretold His death and resurrection, one of His closest disciples took Him aside and rebuked Him. "Far be it from you Lord!" exclaimed Peter. "This shall never happen to you." To which Jesus responded, "You are a hindrance to me. For you are not setting your mind on the things of God, but on the things of man" (Matt 16:22–23).

And again in the Garden of Gethsemane, being in such agony about what was just ahead that His sweat fell like great drops of blood, Jesus asked the Father to remove the cup of suffering. But since He was fully submitted to the Father's will, He declared, "Nevertheless, not my will, but yours, be done" (Luke 22:42–44). He endured the cross for the joy set before Him (Hebrews 12:2). That's a long view perspective.

At times this long view must have been agonizing. After all, Jesus was among the most highly visible public figures of His era. Our modern paparazzi would have shown up in full force as the crowds followed Jesus from place to place. At one point, His popularity was unparalleled. He could influence and mobilize large groups of people. He could have commanded a huge follow-ership and invested His energy to create and lead a major political movement. In modern terms, He could have become the first mega-church pastor. But Jesus resisted the lure of stardom (John 6:15). So committed was He to reconciling the world to the Father that Jesus withdrew from the crowds and focused on the Twelve so that the world could be reached. His long-view perspective went far beyond the direct results of his own life. "To bridge this gulf between earthly priorities and heavenly perspective," writes Roger Parrott, "Jesus became the ultimate example of long-view leadership amid the clamor for expedient results."[1]

LONG-VIEW LEADERS IN HISTORY

History is sprinkled with leaders who reflected Jesus' long view. Telling learners in storycentric settings these kinds of stories connects them to their own story, and they see what leading with a long view might look like for them.

Carpus, Papylus, and Agathonice

In the second century after Christ, two men named Carpus and Papylus were brought before a governor in Rome and charged with the "crime" of being Christian. The governor of the district had discovered that they did not celebrate the pagan festivals, and he ordered the men to be arrested. He commanded them to accept the Roman pagan religion, but Carpus and Papylus said they would never worship false gods.

"I am a Christian," declared Carpus, who was a leader in the church. "I honor Christ, the Son of God, who has come in the latter times to save us and has delivered us from the madness of the devil.

I will not sacrifice to these devils." Not even torture could persuade Carpus to change his mind. He simply kept repeating, "I am a Christian and because of my faith and the name of our Lord Jesus Christ I cannot become one of you."

Then the governor turned to Papylus, a wealthy man with many children. "I have served God since my youth," Papylus said. "I have never sacrificed to idols. I am a Christian. You cannot learn anything else from me. There is nothing I can say which is greater or more wonderful than this."[2]

Both Carpus and Papylus were martyred. Tradition holds that they were burned alive. Inspired by their courage, a woman named Agathonice came forward and confessed that she, too, was a Christian. "If I am worthy, I desire to follow in the footsteps of my teachers," she said to the governor, and she was sentenced to the same death as Carpus and Papylus.

As she was being led to the place of execution, Agathonice removed her clothes and gave them to the poor. The crowd grieved when they saw how beautiful she was. "Lord Jesus Christ," she cried as she was hung above the fire, "help me because I am enduring this for your sake."

It was common knowledge at the time that Christians espoused love and peace, served the common good of society, and prayed for the emperor. They demonstrated that they were good citizens of the empire, and neither Carpus, Papylus, nor Agathonice had committed an actual crime. They died because they confessed Jesus as the only Savior and Lord. They knew the Truth and were convinced that Jesus alone was the only way of reconciliation between God the Creator and His creation. The exclusive Lordship of Jesus Christ challenged all other ultimate claims on their lives—including family, wealth, status, power, and Rome itself. They believed that Jesus brooks no rivals. When forced to choose between worshipping Jesus *plus* the emperor or worshipping *only* Jesus, they pledged their allegiance to Jesus alone.

The church through the centuries has stood on the shoulders of a "cloud of witnesses" of men and women like Carpus, Papylus, and Agathonice, who could foresee a future beyond their own lives and were willing to die for it.

Abraham Lincoln

The man generally considered America's greatest president had a long-view perspective. Steven Spielberg's 2012 film *Lincoln* highlights a four-month period of Lincoln's leadership at the end of the Civil War in 1865, when the president was resolved to abolish slavery.

Lincoln had made it clear that he detested the prevailing zeal for the expansion of slavery. "I hate it because of the monstrous injustice of slavery itself," he declared, and "I hate it because it deprives our republican example of its just influence in the world—enables the enemies of free institutions, with plausibility, to taunt us as hypocrites—causes the real friends of freedom to doubt our sincerity."[3]

The president correctly calculated the task before him, and described the Emancipation Proclamation of 1863 as "the central act of his administration." His courageous leadership resulted in the abolition of slavery, a pivotal event of the nineteenth century.

What makes Lincoln's actions even more admirable is that during the emancipation struggle he took an enormous political risk when the outcome was far from certain. Allen Guelzo, Director of the Civil War Era Studies Program at Gettysburg College, explained that Lincoln took a financial gamble in the battle for justice. The price of abolishing the "retrograde institution" of slavery would turn out to be enormous. The Emancipation Proclamation wiped out $3.5 billion of "investment" in slaves—at a time when the entire wealth of the nation amounted to only $16 billion.[4] Imagine any modern-day president proposing legislation that erases nearly 25 percent of the country's gross national product! This kind of leadership can only be explained by a long view.

Scholars have come to a wide range of conclusions about Abraham Lincoln's religious life. He has been variously portrayed as a committed Christian, a wandering agnostic, and even an occultist. Whatever his personal faith, Lincoln firmly believed that giving freedom to slaves would ensure freedom for the free. This was an ambitious goal, and it could not have been achieved had Lincoln focused solely on the short term. In the end, he paid with his very life. He was assassinated by someone who opposed his long-view dream of an America where the freedom of slaves would fortify succeeding generations and unify them against oppression.

William Seward

Often the good work of those who follow the example of Jesus can only be seen over the long haul. Another such leader was William Seward, who served as a New York governor, a US Senator, and Secretary of State under Andrew Johnson. Seward was the front-runner for the Republican presidential nomination in 1860, but some party members viewed him as too radical due to his views on equality. Both Seward and his wife Frances were committed to the abolition of slavery, as well as other types of controversial social reform. There is evidence that they were involved in the Underground Railroad—a network of secret routes and safe houses used by slaves to flee slavery to free states.

Yet Seward is perhaps best known for his purchase of Alaska. As Johnson's Secretary of State, he engineered a deal to pay Russia seven million dollars for this frozen stretch of land far removed from the continental United States. The purchase was ratified in the Senate in 1867, but it earned Seward severe criticism and the decision became known by his fellow lawmakers as "Seward's Folly."

Despite being publicly excoriated for his actions, Seward displayed a resolute long view that was to change the fate and face of the country. Ninety years after the purchase, America officially recognized Alaska as a state, and her vast resources and native people continue to enrich the nation to this day.[5]

When asked what he considered to be his greatest achievement, Seward replied, "The purchase of Alaska—but it will take the people a generation to find it out." He had been willing to do the hard work of leadership by paying less attention to today's headlines and more to the enduring judgment of history. A contemporary of his, Carl Schurz, accurately described Seward as one of those spirits who sometimes will go ahead of public opinion instead of tamely following its footprints.[6]

Sadhu Sundar Singh

Born in 1889 into a Sikh family in Ludhiana, North India, Sundar Singh studied the Sikh and Hindu religions intently during his childhood. His piety as a young boy was known throughout his native state of Punjab.

The death of his mother when he was fourteen threw the teenager into despair and violence. He vented his rage upon Christian missionaries, persecuted Indian converts, and mocked their faith. He bought a Bible and, as his friends looked on, defiantly burned it page by page in his house.

The despair eventually led Sundar to plan his own death. For three days and nights he stayed in his room, crying out on the third night, "Oh God, if there is a God, reveal Yourself to me tonight." His plan was simple. If God did not speak to him before morning, he would go to the railway tracks, lay his head on the rails, and wait in darkness for the 5 AM train from Ludhiana to end his misery.

For seven hours Sundar waited in silence. At 4:45, a bright cloud of light suddenly filled his room and out of the brightness came the face and figure of Jesus. Sundar had been expecting Krishna or one of his own gods, not Jesus. Yet he was certain it was Jesus.

"How long are you going to persecute me?" Jesus asked Sundar in Hindi. "I died for you. For you I gave my life. You were praying to know the right way; why don't you take it? I am the Way."[7]

As a result of this vision, Sundar's life was dramatically changed. He announced his decision to follow Christ to his father, who denounced him. His brother even attempted to poison him. Like the early Christians, Sundar was persecuted not because he believed that Jesus was divine, but because he trusted Jesus as the only way of salvation.

On his sixteenth birthday, Sundar was baptized in the church in Simla in the Himalayan foothills. A year later, in October 1906, he set out on his journey as a new Christian. "I am not worthy to follow in the steps of my Lord," he declared, "but, like Him, I want no home, no possessions. Like Him I will belong to the road, sharing the suffering of my people, eating with those who will give me shelter, and telling all men of the love of God."

Sundar Singh acquired the title of *sadhu* because he was esteemed as a holy man, and his influence would continue to widen throughout his lifetime. But he also suffered arrest and stoning for his bold witness. In 1908 he crossed the frontier into Tibet, where he was stoned as he bathed in cold water because it was believed that "holy men never washed."

In 1929, against the advice of his friends, Sundar determined to make one final journey to Tibet. He was last seen on April 18, 1929, setting off from Simla. Where he went is unknown. Whether he died of exhaustion or reached the mountains remains a mystery. Some say he was murdered and his body thrown into the river.

Sadhu Sundar Singh was a formative figure in the development of the Christian church in the twentieth century. He is often known as the St. Paul of India. His long-view vision of the gospel of Jesus Christ in his beloved land compelled him to imagine a world beyond his own, a world where Christ is Lord of all.

Dietrich Bonhoeffer

A final example of leadership with the long-view perspective was commemorated on July 27, 1945, at the Holy Trinity Church in London.[8] Two months earlier Hitler had taken his own life in a bunker beneath his crumbled capital of Berlin, and the Allies had declared victory in Europe. A memorial service could finally be held for Dietrich Bonhoeffer, the German theologian and anti-Nazi dissident who had died three months previously. The service had been arranged by the Bishop of Chichester, George Bell, who loved the man being honored. The two had met years before the war, when they were engaged in efforts to warn Europe against the designs of the Nazis. They became close friends as they worked together trying to rescue Jews.

Word of Bonhoeffer's death had staggered out of the war's fog so slowly that his family and friends had learned of it only recently. In the church pews were his 39-year-old twin sister, her half-Jewish husband, and their two girls. They had slipped out of Germany before the war, driving at night across the border into Switzerland.

Bonhoeffer's parents were still in Germany. His father had been the country's most prominent psychiatrist before the war. Karl and Paula Bonhoeffer had both opposed the Third Reich from the beginning, and they were proud of their sons for becoming involved in the conspiracy to abolish it. A month earlier, the Bonhoeffers had learned about the death of Klaus, Dietrich's older brother, but about their youngest son they had heard nothing. Then one day a neighbor told them that the next day the BBC would be broadcasting a memorial service in London—*for Dietrich*. That was how they came to know of his death. At the appointed hour, they turned on the radio and sat beside it for the duration of the broadcast.

As the Bonhoeffers took in the hard news that their son was now dead, so too did many English take in the news that the dead German had been a good man. He was a pastor and a theologian, and had only recently become engaged to the woman he loved. Ever so slowly, the world began to understand the life of Dietrich Bonhoeffer.

In the foreword to Bonhoeffer's book *The Cost of Discipleship*, Bishop Bell writes, "Dietrich himself was a martyr many times before he died. . . . He understood what he chose when he chose resistance. . . . He was crystal clear in his convictions . . . he saw the truth and spoke it with a complete absence of fear."[9]

Much has been written about Bonhoeffer in recent times, and he seems to have acquired a romantic aura. Yet his journey was anything but romantic. His gaze was not set on personal fame; instead, it was focused on a world free of tyranny. The end of his life resembled its entire course, and his decisions and priorities reflected his commitment to his Lord and Savior. Until his last breath Bonhoeffer believed that "when Christ calls a man, he bids him come and die." Or, to put it another way, "We who are alive are always being given over to death for Jesus' sake, so that the life of Jesus may be manifested in our mortal flesh" (2 Cor 4:11). This is a high calling for those who would lead with a long-view.

The words of the writer of Hebrews champion those whose examples have been highlighted in this chapter: "Remember your leaders . . . Consider the outcome of their way of life, and imitate their faith" (Heb 13:7–8). The Western leadership climate expects coaches, presidents, and CEOs to produce instant results, but lasting results never come instantly or by focusing on the short term. Down through the centuries, long-view leadership has always been the way to secure the future, and it is what storycentric communities need today.

CHAPTER 9 SUMMARY

- A primary quality of leadership drawn from the leadership of Jesus Christ is a long-view perspective.
- Jesus Christ was centered on fulfilling His Father's will. With this commitment came a long-view perspective; He endured the cross for the joy set before Him.
- Historical examples of long-view leaders including Carpus, Papylus, and Agathonice, Abraham Lincoln, William Seward, Sabhu Sundar Singh, and Dietrich Bonhoeffer continue to inspire us today.

LEADING WITH VIRTUE

The term "virtuous leadership" has become an oxymoron. It does not carry much credibility in popular culture for three reasons: it is difficult to define; it sounds like a throwback to the Victorian era; and there are so few models of leaders operating with consistently virtuous principles. Real virtue is rare among leaders today.

Take for example a leader named Dwayne. He retired after twenty-five years of leadership as the president of a Christian ministry. During his tenure, the ministry had doubled in size and added four new buildings to its physical plant. The general public considered his leadership a success. When Dwayne announced his retirement, the board declared that they would name one of the newly constructed buildings in his honor. Dwayne was well-known for his commitment to "reach the world for Christ." His 47-year marriage was exemplary, and he demonstrated discipline and moderation in his personal finances. He would often refer fondly to his daily spiritual disciplines of prayer and Bible reading, and how he regularly sought God's will regarding important decisions. During his last ten years of active ministry, Dwayne had been invited to serve on boards of several Christian organizations, and other senior executives respected him for his walk with the Lord. For all intents and purposes, Dwayne's personal life seemed to excel, which caused people to say, "Here is a man who follows God."

However, those within the ministry he led observed a different kind of leader. Despite the fact that board policy forbade the practice, Dwayne quietly diverted designated income away from human resources to fund capital campaigns. He carefully guarded the flow of information to board members, and threatened staff with cuts in salary and benefits if they failed to meet his high expectations. When anyone questioned his unilateral executive decisions, they were chastised for not being in step with God's work. Everyone knew to keep silent or resign. High employee turnover did not affect the ministry severely because new recruits were always available in abundant supply. Staff salaries were kept precariously low year after year as Dwayne would tell everyone that their sacrifice was pleasing to God.

Dwayne's public persona as the leader of the organization contrasted sharply with the values he modeled to those closest to him. He was willing to lay aside his personal convictions in the workplace for the sake of "success." Sadly, his behavior mirrors that of far too many Christian leaders who separate their lives from their livelihood.

The inability to integrate one's personal life and public leadership role produces and perpetuates an unfortunate dualism. Leaders who fall into this trap usually don't intend to be duplicitous, but ministry results become the evidence they use to justify their behavior when they experience such role conflict. Like Dwayne, they would never do many of the things in their personal lives that they dismiss as legitimate behavior in their ministry leadership.

THE LEADERSHIP VIRTUE OF JESUS

To illustrate virtuous leadership for storycentric learners, we point them to a scene from the life of Christ. At the Sea of Tiberius, Jesus demonstrated His miraculous power to stretch resources to exceed expenses by feeding five thousand ravenous adults with five barley loaves and two small fish. So incredible was this miracle that the crowd wanted to make Jesus king and get free lunch forever. He was at the pinnacle of His popularity as a leader at this point.

Through a series of questions, we help storycentric learners to see that this event was a poignant moment in Jesus' life and leadership. Two paths lay before Him. He could either take advantage of the popularity and allow the people to crown Him king, or He could choose the less popular path of suffering. The first choice would allow Him to herald a kingdom that could usher in tremendous change and opportunity for the Jewish people. The second option was to put all that aside and make the less popular and less immediately successful choice of suffering. According to conventional logic, the choice was obvious, but Jesus lived in complete obedience to the Father's will and was never swayed by conventional logic. Indeed, He had already "set his face to go to Jerusalem" (Luke 9:51).

Immediately after feeding the multitude, Jesus enlightened them about the true cost of radical discipleship, charging them to work not for food that spoils, but for the enduring food that the Son of Man gives. When they pressed Him for details, He offended their Jewish sensibilities with the notion that they should eat His flesh and drink His blood (John 6:53–56). This kind of statement is certainly not advisable for the leader focused on short-term outcomes! Jesus knew that many would turn away and no longer regard Him as a successful leader. But He also knew that people would never reach the desired destination of heaven without the eternal Bread that He alone could give. That day Jesus made the virtuous choice.

As He had predicted, this decision and the others He made in the months that followed caused many to turn their backs on Him. Jesus' virtue led Him to walk a lonely path and ultimately die alone, deserted even by His closest companions.

Imagine if Jesus had chosen a different path that day. What would the church look like in the twenty-first century? Would there even be a church today?

Jesus' example demonstrated that the quality and worth of leadership is not necessarily linked to outward success. Rather, it is to be measured in terms of what a leader intends, believes in, and stands for—in other words, *leadership virtue*. This model points to the need for alignment between internal motives and external leadership behaviors. Jesus' life reflected essential leadership virtue that is measured in kingdom terms.

PERSONAL INTEGRITY

So how do we judge the virtue of a leader? Evangelical writers have addressed the importance of personal integrity for Christ-centered leadership. Authors like Leighton Ford, for example, point us to the character of Jesus and rightly assert that a leader's integrity impacts his or her ability to lead effectively.[1] The implosion in recent times of Bernie Madoff's Ponzi scheme, the David Patraeus sex scandal, the meltdown of evangelical personalities, and the widespread epidemic of child abuse among Catholic clerics demonstrates that a public leadership position is not the place to work out one's own character crisis.

When we talk about personal virtue, we are essentially talking about maintaining integrity in all we say and do. We strive to do this so that when we reach the end of our ministry we will, like Paul, finish well. In his final epistle, written from prison shortly before his death, the Apostle writes, "I have fought the good fight, I have finished the race, I have kept the faith" (2 Tim 4:7).

The master in Jesus' parable of the Talents says "Well done, good and faithful servant" to the one who has carried out and completed his task in a praiseworthy manner (Matt 25:23). What then would we give to hear those words from our Lord on the last day?

Author and seminary professor J. Robert Clinton invested much of his career analyzing why Christian leaders do or do not finish well. He found that only about 30 percent of today's Christian leaders finish well.[2] Think about it. *Only 30 percent!*

Those who do finish well experience ever-deepening intimacy in their relationships with God and with others. They never stop learning and growing, even as mature leaders. They lead with proper spiritual authority, and those who follow them recognize God's hand on their lives. Fully submitted to the Lord, these leaders continue to develop toward their full potential, and are used significantly to advance God's purposes.

Sadly, most leaders do not finish well. As Clinton's research reveals, the majority of Christian leaders are falling short of what God intended for their lives. Be it the abuse of finances or power, the damaging effects of pride, the disastrous consequences of inappropriate sexual behavior, or unresolved family issues, it is clear that each of these matters is related to the leader's personal virtue. In other words, most shortfalls among Christian leaders stem from character flaws rather than professional competence. This is not to say that excellence is not important, but only to assert that Christian leaders are experiencing a severe character crisis.

What causes leaders to fall prey to these personal pitfalls? Why do successful, talented, and bright leaders so often sabotage their professional and personal lives through immoral and destructive behavior? In most cases, the fall from grace is neither sudden nor without warning. On the contrary, the path toward destructive behavior is often a predictable process.

The first step toward this downward spiral is growing self-centeredness. Leaders become increasingly confident about their accomplishments until they start believing that they have all the answers. As a result, they increasingly isolate themselves from others.

When a self-centered leader believes his own press releases, he stops managing his life in a healthy way. He starts to ignore friends and loved ones, and these patterns inevitably produce bad habits—such as eating poorly; overworking without allowing time to rest and recharge; or becoming lazy and plateauing in their personal growth, with little intellectual, emotional, or spiritual renewal.

If this process is left to run its course, the leader will start believing that his or her hard work entitles them to a little self-indulgence, whether it's dabbling in questionable activities, or any of the issues, barriers, and temptations cited above. These missteps often result in fractured relationships, personal breakdown, and ministry implosion.

The way for a leader to avoid finishing poorly is to be aware of how those things that destroy a person's inner world inflict damage step-by-step and day-by-day. The antidote is a deliberate effort to plan and engage in daily activities that renew and replenish spiritual, emotional, relational, and physical health.

Jesus finished well because He led a healthy life in all respects, which enabled Him to fulfill what the Father had given Him to do (John 17:4). This goal is within the reach of every leader who follows Christ and desires to emulate His exemplary life and leadership.

PUBLIC VIRTUE

Qualities that reflect personal integrity are indeed foundational for Christ-centered leadership, but what about public virtue?

Storycentric learners often identify with Chuck Noland, the character played by Tom Hanks in *Castaway*, who miraculously survives a plane crash and finds himself marooned on a deserted island. Noland's only focus is to stay alive. Over time he adjusts to existence on the island and figures out ways to maintain his sanity. Four years later, he is rescued and returned home, only to learn that his wife has remarried after losing hope of his survival.

On the lonely island, all things were possible, even an emotional relationship with a volleyball companion named Wilson. But when Noland returns to civilization, he must navigate his way in a complex ethical universe that includes other people.

Through stories like *Castaway*, storycentric learners can ponder how public virtue, unlike personal integrity, is fundamentally a communal exercise. In other words, leadership virtue that is public in nature assumes personal integrity but demands more than that. It is an attempt to work out the rights and obligations we have and share with others.

Leadership virtue has to do with developing standards for judging the conduct of one person whose behavior affects another. It tries to find a way to protect one person's individual rights and needs against and alongside those of others. At the very least, good leadership virtue intends no harm and respects the rights of all affected, while a lack of leadership virtue willfully or negligently tramples on the rights and interests of others.

A discussion of personal integrity and public virtue, however, is not complete without looking at the components of humility and prudence.

Leadership Humility

Humility has been an integral component of leadership virtue since biblical times, but it was not always so admired. Ancient Mediterranean civilizations pursued honor and avoided shame at all costs. Honor was the ultimate asset, shame was the ultimate deficit. Australian writer John Dickson's research found that historians often refer to Egyptian, Greek, and Roman cultures before Christ simply as "honor-shame cultures."[3]

Uppermost in the father's mind in these civilizations was not whether his son would be happy or make money or live morally, but whether he would bring honor to the family. Honor might come through action in a military battle, or advancement through the ranks of society, or even great service to the community. The motivation was not so much the importance of benefiting others; it was the respect and praise that came through activities such as these. Ancient peoples certainly valued justice, social order, and kindness, but the honor one gained—and the shame one avoided— was considered the prize.

Humility was never a virtue before Jesus Christ, who modeled it throughout His earthly life. It burst onstage as a virtue only when His followers attempted to make sense of His crucifixion.[4] Two thousand years of religious art and Christian iconography have unfortunately domesticated our image of the cross, stripping it of its actual shock and horror. Gory details aside, crucifixion was the ancient world's ultimate punishment, the most humiliating of deaths, reserved for political rebels and slaves. The greatest One was willing to be brought to the lowest place the Roman world could envisage: death by crucifixion.

There were only two logical ways to explain this gruesome death: (1) Either Jesus was not the great leader the disciples had originally thought Him to be and this shameful death was evidence of His insignificance; or (2) Jesus had redefined the notion of greatness.

Opponents of early Christianity enthusiastically embraced the first option. In their eyes, Jesus was merely a pretender. But His followers chose the second option. For them, His horrific death was proof that great leadership expresses itself in the noble choice to lower oneself for the sake of others. Paul writes from this ethical perspective:

> Do nothing from selfish ambition or conceit, but in humility count others more significant than yourselves. Let each of you look not only to his own interests, but also to the interests of others. Have this mind among yourselves, which is yours in Christ Jesus (Phil 2:3–5).

The apostle then drives the point home by quoting an early Christian hymn that speaks of Jesus' humility on the cross:

> . . . who, though he was in the form of God, did not count equality with God a thing to be grasped, but emptied himself, by taking the form of a servant, being born in the likeness of men. And being found in human form, he humbled himself by becoming obedient to the point of death, even death on a cross (Phil 2:6–8).

This is nothing less than a humility revolution. In Christ, unprecedented self-emptying and humility encountered self-importance and pride. Honor and shame were turned rightside up when the highly honored Jesus lowered Himself to a shameful cross. And in so doing He became not an object of scorn but one of praise and emulation! The shameful place is now the place of honor. In a relatively short period, both Christians and non-Christians began to use the word "humility" in a positive sense.

In the list of offenses *other* people commit, one that our culture doesn't tolerate for long is arrogance. We simply cannot stomach overtly arrogant people. Arrogance is like sandpaper to sensitive skin. We much prefer humility, and we want even our most exalted leaders and heroes to be modest. When the Miami Heat won the NBA championship in 2012, we liked that Lebron James gave credit to his teammates in the post-game interview. We wouldn't have wanted him to boast, "Hey, what can I tell you, I'm the greatest of all time!"

Obviously, Christians don't have a monopoly on humility. Believers and unbelievers alike are capable of displaying either awe-inspiring humility or revolting arrogance. The point is that humility came to be valued as a consequence of Jesus' dismantling of the honor-shame paradigm. This is why the crucifix, an ancient symbol of shame, can now be found the peak of Mount Everest, the highest point on earth. The One who went to the lowest place has now been exalted above all. Being a Christian is less popular in American culture today than in previous generations, but we continue to embrace humility as a virtue to be admired. At the very least, humility is within the collective DNA of those who desire to lead like our Lord.

Anyone who dares to look within hoping to find in themselves Christ's humility faces an obvious dilemma, for this desirable virtue is elusive. As soon as a person thinks they have it, they probably don't. Conversely, *not* thinking oneself humble is no indication that one *is* humble.

Even though many leaders have naturally strong personalities, which makes them prone to pride, they can purposefully determine to act with humility. Thoughts affect action, but actions can also influence thoughts. Just as counting to ten before exploding in anger helps one develop new ways of dealing with anger, so also forcing oneself to lift the spirits of another or to invite criticism from a subordinate impacts a leader's thinking. Even when one doesn't feel particularly humble, it often helps just to act humbly.

We can gain inspiration from the lives of humble leaders. The biographies of figures such as Mahatma Gandhi and Mother Teresa, to use two examples from the modern era, will edify the attentive reader. Counterexamples are also helpful: reflecting on the lives of people like Caesar, Hitler, and many current CEOs can give us glimpses into the reptilian egos of arrogant leaders. But more important than the lives chronicled in books are the people we actually know who demonstrate humility. Most of us know at least one person with power who places the good of others before themselves. Glenda is one such leader.

Years ago, Glenda began volunteering to teach Scripture classes to middle school-aged boys in her city in Australia. Boys being boys, Glenda's students were not particularly interested in the Scripture lessons—but they were *extremely* interested in the pastries she baked for them. They didn't know or care that their teacher and her husband were wealthy and highly regarded in the community. Most of the boys came from difficult home environments, and Glenda's social status was of little consequence to them. In addition to the scones, Glenda also showered the boys with generous doses of patience.

Although they cared little for the lessons initially, over time they began to develop an interest in Scripture, and eventually nearly all of them committed their lives to Christ. Today several of these boys have grown up to become well-known Christian authors, scholars, and leaders.

I am fortunate to know Glenda personally. Her disciplined, practiced humility has had an immeasurable impact on me. I have benefited greatly from observing her, talking to her, and trying to be a little more like her. With Glenda, it's never about her, and that's one of the qualities that makes her so appealing.

Beyond the fact that humble leaders are just more pleasant to be around, research also demonstrates that humility often has a powerful impact on organizations. Tony Hsieh, the CEO of Zappos, created a company culture based on humility. In the span of a decade, Hsieh took Zappos from a fledgling online clothing store and parlayed it into a billion-dollar business. While Hsieh is certainly not immune to the liabilities of success, his company adheres to a most crucial and unusual value: "Be humble." Every Zappos employee, including every senior leader, goes through rigorous training on the company values, spending weeks working the phones to learn humility. And the quality gets transferred from leaders to associates.

One manager was working for another company when he heard Tony Hsieh speak at a conference. It began raining as the participants were getting ready to leave—and at the door of the conference center stood the CEO of Zappos, handing out ponchos! The manager in question had never seen such service from a senior leader. That day he decided he wanted to work for Tony Hsieh.

Now under the Amazon umbrella, Zappos continues to provide a laser beam of light through the organizational fog that paralyzes so many.[4] I don't know Hsieh's personal views on the Christian faith, but the kind of leadership he displays reflects the greatest model of leadership humility throughout the centuries: that of Jesus the Messiah.

Leadership Prudence

Democritus, the ancient Greek philosopher best remembered for his atomic theory of the universe, once said, "Do not trust all men, but trust men of worth; the former course is silly, the latter a mark of prudence."

Prudence has been an essential leadership virtue historically, but the word has largely fallen out of use. Allen Guelzo, the historian mentioned in the section on Abraham Lincoln, wrote that prudence was considered one of the greatest of virtues two thousand years ago. A hundred years ago it was part of moral philosophy, and today it is the punchline of a joke. For people of a certain generation it will forever conjure up the memory of Dana Carvey impersonating George H. W. Bush saying, "Wouldn't be wise; wouldn't be prudent."

Prudence comes from the Latin term meaning insight, foresight, and wisdom. It is the ability to judge between worthy and questionable actions, and it also has a practical component. Aristotle referred to prudence as "practical wisdom, practical judgment."

Prudence is a leadership term. It is often demonstrated in the midst of chaos, confusion, and crisis, by the leader's ability to make their way through murky waters to the right end. Prudence is an intellectual virtue, but it is essentially a moral virtue. The prudent person is one who *does* the good, as opposed to one who merely *knows* the good.

Stacy was trained as a clinical nurse specialist in adult mental health. She headed the Counseling and Community Service department of a large evangelical church, overseeing a paid staff of twelve people with many more volunteers. She and her husband Alex, a church elder and licensed psychologist, also worked together outside the church as Christian psychotherapists in a reputable counseling service. They knew their stuff. They looked like the ideal couple in both the community and the church—except that Alex was having sexual relations with a former patient, and Stacy was abusing prescription medications. Though they knew better, neither acted with prudence. As a result, he ended up losing his license, and she ended up in a drug rehab center.

Prudence is often equated with caution, but there is a difference between the two. For instance, caution is an excellent strategy when crossing a minefield, and a disastrous one during a gold rush. Prudence, on the other hand, is *always* a good strategy.

Prudence is also not the same thing as avoiding mistakes. Churches are full of leaders who are afraid to make mistakes, thus ensuring that their congregations will never move forward and that their own souls will shrivel from fear and avoidance. Neither is prudence hesitation or procrastination. It is not driving in the middle of the road. Prudence takes the appropriate action at the appropriate time.

A good leadership analogy for prudence is shrewdness—the ability to size up a situation and make decisions based on subtle clues. The prudent leader is intuitive, discreet, and able to pick up clues that reveal what his or her followers really need. In His encounter with the Samaritan woman, Jesus could see that although she had come to draw water from the well, her real need was living water for her thirsty soul. He offered it to her, changing her life forever (John 4:4–15). The shrewd leader is also able to detect ulterior motives behind a mask of goodness. Jesus displayed this quality when He refused to answer the Pharisees regarding the authority behind His miracles (Matt 21:23–27).

Several narratives from the Gospels are effective in teaching storycentric learners that Jesus didn't give Himself to everything and everybody. He was prudent in His relationships, with His time, and ultimately with His very life. Most ministry leaders would probably sign up the person who rushes into their office asking, "What must I do to inherit eternal life?" But Jesus looked at the rich young man, loved him, and said, "You lack one thing" (Mark 10:17–22). Most leaders enjoy it when people compliment their ministries, but at the Passover Feast, where many "believed in his name," Jesus "did not entrust himself to them, because he knew . . . what was in man" (John 2:23–25).

Givers and Takers

We've all met leaders who are givers and those who are takers. Takers are those who like to get more from others than they give. They are adept at tilting reciprocity, the interplay of give and take, in their favor. Givers, on the other hand, are other-focused. They attend more to what others need than what they themselves need.

According to a number of studies cited by Wharton professor Adam Grant in his book *Give and Take: A Revolutionary Approach to Success,* giving leaders are often less successful because they are too caring, too trusting, and too willing to forego their own interests for the benefit of others.[5] Research among engineers in California, medical students in Belgium, and salespeople in North Carolina revealed the same patterns: givers litter the ranks of the unsuccessful.

However, it's also the givers that are consistently ranked highest in their professions. As Grant puts it, givers are both the "chumps" and the "champs" of the world. They have greater success in their work because they interact with others differently. For example, they contribute sacrificially to a team and recognize the contribution of their colleagues. Thus they gain the respect of others and don't attract the jealousy that takers often do. Givers are also better at evaluating, developing, and influencing talent than takers.

So what distinguishes givers who are successful from those who are not? Grant found that givers who stand out are those who engage in "sincerity screening." Sincerity screening is the skill of separating out the authentic from those just trying to take advantage. It is another term for prudence. Effective leaders don't give indiscriminately. Rather, they activate their giving based on a savvy perspective on the sincerity of others.

Jesus' giving was consistently discriminate. To one religious leader, He spoke words of life (John 3:1–14). To other religious leaders, He spoke words of condemnation. Early in His ministry, Jesus invited the crowds to "come and see," yet later He seemed to drive them away. In His encounters with Zacchaeus, the lawyers, the Pharisees, the Sanhedrin, the woman with the issue of blood, the one caught in adultery, and the crowds, Jesus gave Himself to others with a keen eye on their authentic desire for help. Even when it came to laying down His life, He did so at the time of His choosing, with full awareness of the circumstances.

Prudence—the capacity to face reality squarely and to act resolutely—makes a person an effective leader. It was memorably displayed by a software salesman named Todd Beamer on September 11, 2001. That morning, Beamer boarded United Flight 93 in Newark with plans to attend a routine business meeting in San Francisco. But less than an hour after takeoff, a group of hijackers led by Zaid Samir Jarrah commandeered the cockpit with the intent to use the jet as a missile of war against the United States. As the passengers were herded to the back of the plane, Beamer used his credit card to place a call from the phone on the back of a seat and was connected with a telephone operator named Lisa Jefferson. He told her what was happening, and she in turn relayed to him the grim news that other hijacked flights had already crashed into the Twin Towers and the Pentagon.

In that moment, Beamer quickly sized up the dire situation, and steadily quoted over the phone the Lord's Prayer. Then he told Jefferson that he and the other passengers were planning to "jump on" the hijackers and fly the plane into the ground before the hijackers could follow through with their plan. According to Jefferson, Beamer's last audible words as he led others toward destiny were, "Are you guys ready? Okay. Let's roll." Spoken by a man facing certain death, these words would inspire millions in the aftermath of 9/11. In America, it became something of a catch-phrase for courageous action.

As is evident from the examples of Christ and people like Todd Beamer, prudence allows one to accurately assess a situation, decide with discernment, and act with resolve. Leadership prudence is both insight and foresight. It is an acquired habit to make immediate decisions and take action in light of longer-range consequences. As such, it's a quality any Christ-centered leader who strives for excellence will want to cultivate.

THE DILEMMA OF VIRTUE: SLICING THE ONION

This all sounds good and true, but here is the dilemma. While most Christian leaders agree with the need for personal integrity in one's private life, many of these same people function as if personal integrity and public virtue exist in different realms. Whether this inconsistency arises from insufficient understanding or a lack of good role models, many behave as if "business is business," as though the standards involved in running an organization are different from, more important than, and perhaps even antithetical to the principles and practices they adhere to in their private lives. Separating personal integrity and public virtue may cost prestige, position, and profits, but it will lead a person down a slippery slope.

God indeed blesses some leaders with financial, political, and positional success. However, we cannot expect every decision and action of a virtuous leader to produce a "successful" outcome. Although we can find biblical examples like Joshua who were both moral and successful, the Scriptures also demonstrate that virtuous leadership does not always produce consequences that are popularly regarded as successful. For instance, Moses never saw the Promised Land. Jeremiah was "the weeping prophet." John the Baptist, described as "the voice of one crying out in the wilderness," was beheaded for preaching the truth without compromise. The Apostle Paul was beaten, imprisoned, and eventually martyred for his witness.

Jesus' three years of leadership would have been considered a dismal failure by most modern organizational measures. To the Roman politicians who never understood His mission, as well as to the overwhelming majority of ordinary people, Jesus was at best a harmless rebel and at worst a dangerous revolutionary. This latter designation was doubtless a factor in His being labeled a criminal and subsequently crucified.

Those leaders who prioritize success above all else are at risk of compromising their personal standards. To consistently stand on higher ground, one must embrace virtuous leadership as a worthy goal in and of itself.

Aristotle said that character is the most crucial and the most elusive element of leadership. The root of the word *character* comes from the Greek word for "engraving". As applied to human beings, character refers to the enduring marks in our personalities that include our inborn talents as well as the learned and acquired traits imparted to us by life and experience. These engravings define us, set us apart, and motivate our behavior.

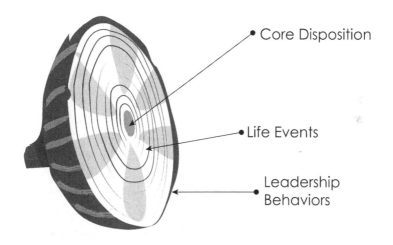

Core Disposition

Life Events

Leadership Behaviors

To help storycentric people see how these character "engravings" work, we describe leadership as having the characteristics of an onion.[6] This is an analogy men and women from most cultures will readily understand, given how common the onion is.

The two distinguishing characteristics of the onion are its layers and its strong aroma. Assuming that the skin represents observable leadership behaviors, the journey of self-understanding begins at the innermost layer and moves outward to the layer that others can see. A leader's behaviors rest on the less visible and less examined layers of self that have been formed through a combination of the core dispositions inherited from parents (core layer) and the values the leader has developed through the evolution of events over a lifetime (middle layers). Jesus was keenly aware of His less visible layers (His core identity and the source of His value that empowered Him to serve others selflessly).

Anyone who has cut an onion knows the discomfort the process involves: eyes become red and irritated and start to sting as tears develop. Similarly, peeling back the layers of the inner self can also be uncomfortable for a leader. It is not easy to take an honest inventory of the good and the bad, the bright spots and the shadows in our life. The shadow side acts on our need for self-preservation. Fear of rejection makes us want to control how others see us instead of letting them see us as we really are.[7] Getting in touch with the shadow side can be unsettling, but mature development of leadership character can only come from understanding every layer.

As the Scandinavian philosopher Kierkegaard famously said, "Life must be lived forwards, but can only be understood backwards." Virtuous leadership calls for a grace-filled look backward at the less visible layers to understand who we are, who we are not, and *why*. It requires a humble acceptance of our strengths and a patient acknowledgement of our weaknesses, upon which is founded a reformation of future leadership behaviors. This requires a forward-leaning, daily embracing of Christ's transforming grace and power, which is the fountainhead of virtuous leadership.

THE LENS OF CONSCIENCE

Leading with virtue additionally requires a conscience that has become well-tuned by heeding the Holy Spirit's counsel through honest feedback from trusted friends and colleagues. The noted psychologist Eric Fromm, who suffered the evils of Nazism, said that "the paradoxical and tragic situation of man is that his conscience is weakest when he needs it most."[8]

Our conscience is intended to act like a judge, alternatively accusing and defending us. When the lens of conscience is clear, its job is to tap us on the shoulder and point out whether our walk matches our talk. In a perfect world, conscience acts as a safeguard to let us know that our leadership is on track or, alternatively, as an arbiter to tell us, "You're drifting off course."

The lens of our conscience bends with the warp and woof of life. The more it bends, the harder it is for leaders and organizations to "see" the difference between black, white, and gray. The conscience will keep humming along, but with a distorted lens, it will lead us off course. Unfortunately, leadership gets complex and messy. At such times, leaders with a distorted lens will do the wrong thing—character assassination, power plays, manipulation—and then disregard correction, defend their actions, or play the role of a victim of circumstances.

The problem is with the lens. Since the lens of individual conscience is usually a bit blurred, leaders can deceive themselves. We need the "eyeglasses" of others in order to see clearly. I doubt leaders intentionally live by a distorted lens. They don't wake up and say, "I'm going to be a jerk today." They don't drive to work thinking, "How can I bring destruction in the lives of people?" But regardless of their intentions, that is what often happens.

In 2002, companies like WorldCom, Enron, Sunbeam, Adelphia, and Qwest dominated the media because of their accounting irregularities. As a result, millions of shareholders' dollars lost value, causing many to suffer. How did this happen? The leaders of these companies had over time developed faulty lenses of conscience, which allowed them to justify their actions.

Christian organizations have also paid a high price at the hands of unbridled visionaries and unprincipled pragmatists. Often these leaders claim to have heard the voice of God, but the lens of their conscience is blurred—if not altogether shattered.

Reality Distortion Field (RDF) is another term that describes the faulty lens of individual conscience. According to Walter Isaacson's biography of Apple Computer co-founder Steve Jobs, RDF was originally coined to describe Jobs' ability to convince himself and others to accomplish almost anything with a mix of charisma, bravado, marketing, and persistence.[9]

With RDF, Jobs was able to influence others' sense of proportion and scales of difficulties. He made (often forced) colleagues to believe that the task at hand was possible. For example, he would design the look of a device, then demand that the company's engineers accomplish the herculean task of fitting the device's components within the design. Or he would publicly announce that a product would be available by a certain deadline that seemed impossible to meet. Jobs' success was due in no small part to his iron will and his incredible capacity to convince others to excel.

But there were major problems with Jobs' RDF. While his charm, giftedness, and sheer genius commanded great admiration, and even though he blessed the world with the Mac, the iPhone, the iPad, and iTunes, many of his competitors, coworkers, friends, and family absorbed the brunt of his abuse when they did not buy into his vision. In the end, cancer claimed Jobs' life prematurely in part because he thought his RDF would overcome his pancreatic tumor. His lens was blurred in the crucial decision-making moments of his life.

Many leaders in storycentric communities relate to Jobs' passion to "make a dent in the universe," although most possess neither his genius nor his charm so will never attain his titan status. But many of us share his problem with the lens of conscience. If individual conscience is the only lens through which we see reality, we are a soft target for self-deception.

We are easy prey to delusion if we take counsel only within ourselves and neglect outside help. Leaders and organizations make a grave error when they try to decipher their conscience on their own. An essential part of the solution may not be deeper soul-searching or longer prayer vigils, but developing an ear and a process for receiving outside signals from the broader community that can inform our collective conscience. One of the most critical decisions a person will ever make as a leader is the lens he or she selects through which to see reality.

"Faithful are the wounds of a friend," wrote King Solomon (Prov 27:6). Real friends can be painful because they help us decipher reality. They help us see with a clear conscience.

Discerning alternative voices has always been invaluable for healthy leaders and organizations. To maintain leadership virtue, we need to expand our leadership circle to include those who can discern whether we are functioning with a clear view of reality. The idea is not to marginalize their input but rather to institutionalize their contribution.

Conscience is a key characteristic that changes the game. We simply cannot get around it or over it. Our commitment to a clear lens of conscience that passes through communion with God and community with others usually determines our leadership effectiveness both in our personal integrity and in our public virtue.

If you aspire to be a Christ-centered leader, be aware that you will face a giant obstacle: your own conscience. As the prophet Jeremiah long ago told us, our conscience is easily deceived (Jer 17:9). It's why the British social reformer William Wilberforce urged his teenaged daughter to cultivate a clear conscience by accustoming herself to self-suspicion. Wilberforce had learned from years of leadership in the political trenches that a distorted conscience is the culprit behind corruption.

Ministries need Christ-like leaders who exemplify both personal integrity and public virtue with humility and prudence. As we have seen in this chapter, discerning alternative voices is a primary means to achieve this kind of leadership virtue.

CHAPTER 10 SUMMARY

- Virtuous leadership is concerned with the integration of one's personal life and public leadership role.
- While personal integrity is foundational, leadership virtue has to do with developing standards for judging the conduct of one person whose behavior affects another.
- Humility is a core quality of leadership virtue; Jesus ushered in a humility revolution that has continued to impact the world.
- Another primary leadership virtue is prudence, the ability to judge between worthy and questionable actions. Leadership prudence is practical wisdom; it moves beyond knowing to doing. Taking a cue from Jesus' model, giving leaders who are prudent are more effective.
- Leaders who understand their core "engravings" are more likely to experience the transforming power of Christ in their leadership.
- Leadership virtue also requires a clear lens of conscience that becomes more well-tuned by heeding the Holy Spirit's counsel through honest feedback from trusted friends and colleagues.

11
LEADING OTHERS TOWARD THEIR POTENTIAL

Jesus had one major leadership priority: to develop leaders for the future. The disciples He chose were an unlikely collection of future church leaders, but He spent three years mentoring them. And as the time for His crucifixion drew nearer, He devoted most of His time and energy toward cultivating them for their forthcoming ministry. Jesus did not have an earthly position of delegated authority, so His leadership of others was not accomplished through strong-arm coercion, positional control, or constituted power. Rather, people had a choice to follow Him or to reject His invitation and turn away. He always led by influencing people and building into them through authentic relationships.

Our freedom to choose was one of God's most profound displays of true leadership. From the beginning of time, relationship rather than control has been God's modus operandi with the human race. The entire Bible, from Genesis to Revelation, tells the story of a God who desires relationship with the people He created. That our God leads in a way not based on power or position is reflected in the fact that Jesus was born into a family of low socioeconomic status. A restored relationship with God that is dependent on a person's choice is central to the gospel message. Without exception, Jesus led only people who wanted to follow Him.

AUTHENTIC RELATIONSHIPS

The Gospels are filled with images of Jesus' commitment to authentic relationships. To communicate this pivotal principle to storycentric learners, we often recount that great moment of Jesus' leadership when He called a fisherman named Simon to follow Him.

On one occasion, while the crowd was pressing in on him to hear the word of God, he was standing by the Lake of Gennesaret, and he saw two boats by the lake, but the fishermen had gone out of them and were washing their nets. Getting into one of the boats, which was Simon's, he asked him to put out a little from the land. And he sat down and taught the people from the boat.

And when he had finished speaking, he said to Simon, "Put out into the deep and let down your nets for a catch."

And Simon answered, "Master, we toiled all night and took nothing! But at your word I will let down the nets." And when they had done this, they enclosed a large number of fish, and their nets were breaking. They signaled to their partners in the other boat to come and help them. And they came and filled both the boats, so that they began to sink.

But when Simon Peter saw it, he fell down at Jesus' knees, saying, "Depart from me, for I am a sinful man, O Lord." For he and all who were with him were astonished at the catch of fish that they had taken, and so also were James and John, sons of Zebedee, who were partners with Simon.

And Jesus said to Simon, "Do not be afraid; from now on you will be catching men." And when they had brought their boats to land, they left everything and followed him." (Luke 5:1–11)

Prior to this, Luke records that Jesus had visited Simon's home and healed his sick mother-in-law (Luke 4:38–39). Thus Jesus was building a relationship with Simon even before this event played out by the Lake of Gennesaret. From the start, He was leading through relationship.

The night before Jesus called Simon to be a fisher of men, Simon and his fellow fishermen had worked a long and fruitless shift. Time after time they had thrown their nets into the water and held the ropes hopefully. All night they waited for a tug that would signal them to haul up their catch, but it never happened, and their boat was still empty at dawn.

After loaning the boat to Jesus for an impromptu teaching session, Simon was preparing to go home when Jesus instructed him to push out and let down the nets one more time. I wonder if Simon thought, "What do you think we have been doing all night? We have let down the nets hundreds of times. Rabbi, I was glad to loan you my boat for your teaching. And you did give an excellent speech. But we are the fishermen. We know what we're doing. Preachers don't know *everything*!"

Nevertheless, Simon gave Jesus the benefit of the doubt and did as Jesus instructed. He may have thought, "If he could heal my mother-in-law, then maybe there's hope for us, too." When the fishermen let down the nets this time, nearly every fish in the lake jumped into the nets! Thus, in preparation for what was about to unfold, Jesus demonstrated not only His ability to perform miracles, but also His concern for the men's practical needs.

What happened next is sometimes overlooked in the narrative. When Simon recognized the power of this man who was sharing the boat with him, he immediately fell to his knees and cried out, "Lord, go away from me, for I am sinful."

Jesus could have replied, "I couldn't agree with you more, Simon. You're *horribly* sinful!" And from the perspective of a holy God, this response would have been correct. But instead of that, Jesus said, "Don't be afraid. From now on you'll fish for people." In other words, He was saying, "Simon, you are important to me. I believe in you. Your purpose lies far beyond this boat and these nets. Follow me, and your tomorrows will exceed your wildest dreams."

What leaders really believe about those they lead will become evident before long. In calling himself sinful, Simon proved that he had an accurate view of himself before the Son of God; but Jesus saw in him the raw ingredients of a future apostle of priceless worth.

And what happened next shows the history-changing impact of this: Simon and the others pulled their boats to shore, left everything, and followed Jesus.

Did the fishermen respond to Jesus' call because He had positional power over them? No. He didn't command or control them. Rather, Jesus influenced them through relationship and by speaking to the potential He saw in them. So inspired was Simon by this relational influence that Jesus' vision became his own vision, His purpose Simon's purpose. And all because Jesus had believed in him.

Apart from everything else, Jesus must have been a great friend. He was sensitive to people's needs, and He fostered relationships by spending time with people. No doubt He could have accessed His divine power to instantly transport Himself from one ministry location to another, but He opted for "economy fare" in order to spend time with those He loved and valued. As they walked the dusty footpaths together, they talked about important things that don't usually come up during a power lunch. Jesus listened to them, responded to their questions, and told them many stories. He would debrief with them after their efforts to minister to others and explain things when they didn't get it all. He shared with them the inside scoop about the end times. He debriefed with them after their efforts to minister to others.

Jesus loved His disciples to such an extent that just before the crucifixion He said, "No longer do I call you servants, for the servant does not know what his master is doing; but I have called you friends, for all that I have heard from my Father I have made known to you" (John 15:15). And afterwards, He never gave up on them because they had denied or deserted Him when He needed them most. Through true friendship, Jesus profoundly shaped the lives of His disciples, which in turn profoundly shaped the course of history.

IMPACT OF GLOBAL TRENDS ON LEADERSHIP

Instead of Jesus' example of relationship building, we more often see the exertion of power among ministry leaders today. Instead of influence and encouragement, we more often see overt leadership control and micromanagement. The kind of leadership Jesus modeled is crucial in the present age because of three global trends that are shaping the leadership climate both inside and outside the church: (1) acute skepticism, (2) access to information, and (3) altered contracts.[1]

Acute Skepticism

The current workforce has greater skepticism toward leaders today because incompetent and unethical leaders have stained the public's consciousness in every sphere—be it politics, military, business, education, or ministry. One barometer that reflects the current social attitude is a bumper sticker that reads, "Don't vote—it will only encourage them." In general, people are more pessimistic about leaders' capacity or commitment, so they are far less eager to follow any leader with whom they do not have a relationship.

Access to Information

The unprecedented access to information has changed public perception of leadership authority. For instance, more computing power is embedded on my iPhone than existed on the entire planet in 1950! With access to information only a keystroke away, power has shifted away from those with titles to those with technology, even in the storycentric world. More than any other force, this power shift is responsible for the flattening of hierarchies and the movement of the center of gravity away from powerful bosses to empowered people. In our globally connected village, influential relationships rather than organizational charts are the primary route through which people are influenced today.

Altered Contracts

The rules of engagement have drastically changed people's loyalty to the organization and its leaders. Back in the 1990s, employers and employees alike redefined the social contract. Large companies like

IBM shed jobs at a record pace. As permanent jobs were replaced with a contingent workforce, people's loyalty to the organization has largely become a relic of the past. Nevertheless, leaders in this challenging environment can still engender relational trust where people are treated with dignity and respect regardless of the circumstances.

These global trends point toward a desperate need among Christian ministries for leaders who influence people through healthy relationships. But all too often our leaders take their cues from Nurse Ratched in the 1962 film *One Flew Over the Cuckoo's Nest.*

The story is about a man sentenced to prison for petty crimes. To avoid prison, R. P. McMurphy, played by a young Jack Nicholson, feigns insanity thinking that serving his sentence in a mental ward would be easier than serving time in a prison. So McMurphy is committed to a facility for the mentally ill. Upon arrival, he encounters his worst nightmare in the person of the head nurse of the ward.

In her white pressed uniform, Nurse Ratched rules the patients with an iron hand. She is a strong and capable professional who has chosen a career in the mental health industry. However, under the guise of doing "good" for them, she punishes free expression and is intolerant of those who question her authority. Nurse Ratched really believes she is doing the right thing, but her hideous control destroys her patients' spirits and results in their turning violent, leading to bloodshed and eventually suicide.

This illustration may seem a bit over the top, but the image isn't far from reality. Ministry leaders, who have chosen a professional vocation intended to express care and compassion, often end up commanding, controlling, and condemning those they lead. As Henri Nouwen put it, "Much Christian leadership is exercised by people who do not know how to develop healthy, intimate relationships and have opted for power and control instead."[2] Like the religious leaders of Jesus' day, much of what today's ministry leaders believe and do in the realm of power and control has been borrowed not from the Scriptures, but from the surrounding secular institutions.

Sometimes our ministries overlook those who influence others through relationships and instead assign people to leadership positions who manipulate through power and control. We have confused institutional power with influential leadership. By blending the two we have made them appear the same, whereas they are in fact diametrically opposed. An epidemic of power leadership is rife in ministry organizations today. This style is not helping expand the kingdom. Rather, it is driving people away from the church and Christian organizations, and hindering our witness in the world. Almost as tragic is the fact that power leaders are so common that we've all but lost our ability to identify them.

Power and Control

Ministry leaders are called to be managers of power and control. Some types of control are good and necessary; for example, without boundaries and rails a locomotive won't stay on the track. But like Nurse Ratched, control can take on a variety of destructive forms— such as pressuring followers into uniformity, shaming individuals for creative thinking, withholding association from those who don't meet our standards, and micromanaging capable people.

The appropriate application of power and control is a reality that every leader faces; the struggles and dilemmas of effective leadership are continually before us. We do well to keep in mind the following principles related to power.

1. Every leader is a steward of power, because leadership always comes with power.

The exercise of power is not the same as the practice of leadership. As author Jim Collins says in *Good to Great And the Social Sectors*, "If I put a loaded gun to your head, I can get you to do things you might not otherwise do, but I've not practiced leadership; I've exercised power."[3] If people follow because they have no choice, then that's not leading.

2. The legitimate use of power can unleash much that is good.

Power that energizes people is rarely power that commands and controls them. When Frances Hesselbein became CEO of the Girl

Scouts of America, she inherited a volunteer force of 650,000 and a complex governance structure. (For example, each local Girl Scout council had its own governing board.) In addition, Hesselbein had to deal with the brutal crises facing girls in modern America, such as teen pregnancy and substance abuse. She combated these problems by producing materials on sensitive issues and creating proficiency badges in topics like math, technology, and computer science. She sought to reinforce the idea that girls are valuable, capable, and should take control of their own lives. She did not force changes down people's throats, but simply gave the local Girl Scout councils the opportunity to make changes at their own discretion. And most of them did. When asked how she got all this done without executive power, Hesselbein said, "Oh, you always have power, if you just know where to find it. There is the power of inclusion, and the power of language, and the power of shared interests, and the power of coalition."[4] What wise words these are!

3. Power can either create or destroy; it is almost never neutral.

Power used wisely has enormous potential for the kingdom. God's power brought the universe into being and raised Jesus from the dead. That's creative power. But Adam and Eve's sin was destructive power. They wanted to be more, know more, and have more. They were not content to be creatures; they wanted to be gods. Similarly, most leaders struggle with the feeling that they never have quite enough power. Nothing touches leaders more profoundly, for good or ill, than power. Power is like drinking salt water: the more you drink the thirstier you get.

4. The most damaging result of destructive leadership power is ruptured relationships.

Destructive leadership power destroys dialogue. It breaks trust. Adam and Eve's will to power caused a break in their perfect relationship with God and with one another. King Saul's will to power ruptured his relationship with David. David's will to power destroyed his integrity and cost Uriah his life. And Lucifer's will to power cost him his relationship with God for all eternity.

5. Power can be especially destructive in the service of religion.
The destructive use of religious power can damage in a way that no other power can. The current spread of terrorism by religious extremists demonstrate that those who become a law unto themselves, and at the same time take on a mantle of piety, are particularly corruptible and destructive. When leaders are convinced that their voice is the voice of God, they assume inappropriate authority and use it to their own ends. Those ministry leaders who are not accountable are most susceptible to this tragic misuse of power.

Unhealthy Control

What drives leaders to wield unhealthy control? Usually it is *fear*. Many leaders fear the expectations they perceive others might have of them, and they fear their own responsibilities and expectations. Controlling leaders are afraid that they will appear ordinary and inadequate unless others perform exactly as they require, so they demand unquestioning loyalty and obedience. They simply can't allow for freedom of expression or diversity of opinions that naturally flow out of real relationships.

As I was writing the final words of this section, my phone rang with the sad news that a friend and former colleague was fired by the Christian ministry he led. In many ways, this man had all the right gifts: eloquence, education, energy, and an impressive database of potential donors. He clearly has a passion to communicate the message of Christ to the world, and he worked hard to align the ministry organization with the vision he believed God had given him. But somewhere along the way he became alienated from his colleagues. Ambition was his commanding officer; power and control were his ammunition. His personal and professional relationships wore thin under the strain. Those close to him knew his life and leadership were unraveling. But he had stopped listening to others and took counsel only from himself until it was too late.

In our fast-paced world, doing the work of leadership can actually become an assault on the pursuit of grace-based relationships that drew us into Christian ministry in the first place. If left unchecked, it can eventually lead into the shadows of the destructive use of power and an irrational dependency on control.

You and I have real work to accomplish with real leadership responsibilities in ministry organizations with real expectations. In light of these enormous challenges, now is an opportune time to follow the less popular but worthier example of Jesus, who changed the world through influential relationships, not power and control.

Robert Frost's poem "The Road Not Taken" closes with these famous lines:

> Two roads diverged in a wood, and I—
> I took the one less traveled by,
> And that has made all the difference.

May these lines inspire us as ministry leaders to take the less traveled road and serve those we lead as our Lord did.

HIDDEN POTENTIAL

Several years ago a friend gave me a picture book that promised to enable the viewer to "see what is invisible." It was my first experience with stereograms, those incredible 3D images that look like a collection of jumbled shapes and colors until the eye adjusts its focus. At first it was frustrating. I worked hard to train myself to look beyond the two-dimensional surface; I literally had to see in another way. It took a while but once I did, all of a sudden the hidden image "appeared" in 3D right before my eyes!

Adjusting our focus to see into a stereogram is an appropriate metaphor for leadership. Ministry stakeholders place demands upon leaders to succeed—sometimes *at all costs*. This pressure motivates leaders to subconsciously view their associates as mere cogs in the organization's machinery, useful only insofar as they contribute to the organization's success. But this is two-dimensional seeing. What we need are eyes to see the people we lead in 3D, to look beyond their immediate usefulness and towards their potential. We need to see the hidden "image."

In 1969, a troubled man named Hunter Adams voluntarily committed himself into a mental institution, where he found that helping his fellow patients gave him a sense of purpose. This inspired him to become a medical doctor, a dream he was fortunately able to realize. Through a series of events at Virginia Medical University, the non-conformist Adams challenged the faculty and students to see their patients as people, not problems. He argued that even death should be treated with dignity, even humor. The 1998 film *Patch Adams*, starring Robin Williams, is based on his story.

In the movie, Adams' life is changed by an encounter with a fellow patient in the mental institution. Arthur, who used to be a noted mathematician, is often seen wandering about the ward holding up his fingers and yelling, "Four." Attendants assume he has lost his mind.

One day Adams approaches Arthur and asks, "Fingers. What's the answer?"

Noting Adams' sincerity, Arthur responds, "Hold up your (four) fingers. How many do you see?"

"There are four fingers, Arthur," says Adams.

"No!" retorts Arthur. "You're focusing on the problem. Never focus on the problem. Look beyond the fingers. Look at me. Now how many do you see?"

Adams adjusts his focus and exclaims, "Eight!"

"Yes, eight," says Arthur. "Now you see what no one else sees. You see what others choose not to see . . . You see the whole world anew, each day. I fancy you're well on the way."

This way of seeing can change our lives, our leadership, and the people we serve. Yet for most leaders, seeing in 3D doesn't come naturally—just as I have to train myself to see beyond the surface each time I return to those stereograms. But it gets easier with time and practice, and it's well worth the effort. As we adjust our vision, hidden potential appears right before our eyes.

What set Jesus' leadership apart was His capacity to "see" and develop His followers' potential. He saw people as God's image-bearers. He saw the future fueled by their collective, Spirit-empowered genius, and consistently demonstrated His unflinching commitment for them to reach their highest kingdom potential. Whereas His contemporaries prioritized their own interests and well-being, Jesus invested in the interests and well-being of others.

The radical priority that His followers grow to their maximum kingdom potential was at the heart of Jesus' life and ministry. He never traveled very far from the place where He was born. He never published a bestseller, never made a lot of money, and never held a prominent position. Instead, He gave Himself to the task of reproducing His heart into those who would carry the torch after His departure. He set His vision on the future, when those He had developed would catalyze a movement to change the world.

On the night before His crucifixion, Jesus foretold the coming of the Holy Spirit, who would enable the disciples to do even greater things than they had seen Jesus do. Later, when He appeared to them just before His ascension, He announced that they would be filled with the Holy Spirit to be witnesses. Sure enough, after the Day of Pentecost, the disciples' leadership influence resulted in the conversion of thousands and the birth of a church that has already lasted twenty-one centuries! They were able to reach far beyond Jesus' ministry landscape, but they couldn't have done it without first being developed and empowered by Him.

The dream of greater influence through developing others must also have motivated Barnabas to endorse Saul to the apostles and develop him to become the first great missionary to the Gentiles. And it is this same dream that compels leaders in our day to seize the opportunity to develop others so that the glory of God may fill the whole earth.

Most people have God-given potential that is merely waiting for a bit of encouragement to bloom fully. Businessman and writer Max De Pree tells a story about his granddaughter who was born with special challenges. Once when she came to visit him she said, "Grandpa, would you like to see me run?"

Said De Pree, "I must tell you, my heart jumped as I thought to myself, 'This little girl can hardly walk. How is she going to run?' But like a good grandparent, I said, 'Yes, I'd like to see you run.'"

With that, the young girl waddled over to one side of the room and started to run, right across in front of his desk and directly into the side of the refrigerator. It knocked her on her back, and there she lay, spread-eagled on the floor with a big grin on her face.

De Pree was filled with concern. "Honey, you've got to learn to stop," he said.

At that, she looked up and said, "But Grandpa, I'm learning to run!"

Handle With Care

Human potential that is catalyzed by encouragement is a combustible combination for good. But human potential is also a fragile thing, a fact that struck me powerfully one Sunday afternoon.

I was the guest speaker at a small church and went to the pastor's home for lunch after the service. As we sat at the table, I could tell that this meal was different from usual. The pastor's wife had set out the special napkins and silverware; the three children were on their best behavior.

The older son caught my attention. He was a tall, lanky kid with cerebral palsy. After we'd become acquainted, I said, "Alan, what subjects do you like in high school?"

"Algebra," he replied with a smile. "I love Algebra."

I was intrigued. "What do you want to do after you graduate from high school?"

Haltingly, he said, "I-I want to be a math teacher."

"So where do you want to go to college?" I asked, at which point his father jumped in.

"Alan's handicapped," he said curtly. "He's not going to college."

No sooner had those words been spoken than the light in Alan's face drained away. The boy who had told me about his love for Algebra with such animation remained silent for the rest of the meal.

The common folk in Jesus' day were oppressed in various ways and for various reasons. Their potential was undervalued, and they were not encouraged to reach for what is possible. But Jesus saw the potential in people and nurtured it. For example, He saw a despised tax collector as a future Gospel writer, a diamond in the rough brimming with latent promise. A hotheaded, unschooled fishermen was, in Jesus' eyes, a leader of the early church. He envisioned a downtrodden woman who had led an immoral life as the steward of the kingdom message in her village.

This priority of Jesus' ministry, characterized by His leading people through authentic relationship toward their potential, is distinct from all other leadership models that are quickly discarded if they don't produce the expected results for the leader or the organization. Jesus had only one model. He did not seem to have a backup plan, should His followers fail to reach their potential. He had one primary focus: to draw out the potential of those He called disciples . . . and friends. Those who lead in this way do so with no guaranteed outcome, but only with assurance that it is the right way to lead. There is no more life-changing leadership priority than this.

I have served in various ministry leadership positions over the years. Seen from a human perspective, some of my posts have turned out to be more productive than others. But as I look at the ups and downs of these ministry assignments in the rearview mirror, one common theme emerges: within a short time after my departure, the ministry organization inevitably changed. Often the priorities that were so important to me were placed on the back burner or were abandoned altogether. My efforts to champion goals and strategies to advance the ministry's impact usually have a short shelf life after I leave.

On the other hand, the energy I have invested in developing people has had a far more enduring effect. I believe that in the final analysis, my lasting contribution will be the men and women in whom I have invested, who will carry the leadership torch after my ministry is over and forgotten. As someone has said, "More time spent with fewer people equals greater impact for God." That principle was true in Jesus' life; I am finding it to be true in mine.

CHAPTER 11 SUMMARY

- A fundamental distinguishing characteristic of Christ-centered leadership is the commitment to prioritize others' highest kingdom potential over one's own personal success.
- Jesus demonstrated that this commitment to others' highest Kingdom potential is rooted in the leader's authentic relationships with others.
- Three global trends (acute skepticism, access to information, and altered contracts) have created a critical need for Christ-centered leaders who are committed to others' growth and well-being.
- The appropriate application of power and control is a reality that every responsible leader stewards with care.
- A commitment to others requires seeing hidden potential, and treating the developing leader with care and respect.

12
CHRIST-CENTERED LEADERSHIP APPLIED

The previous chapters describe the characteristics of a Christ-centered leader and examine both the scope of leadership development and effective processes for developing leadership. We also took a fresh look at the impact and place of story, not only among the unreached peoples, but also within literate societies—for story impacts us all. The images and principles that have been presented about cultivating Christ-centered leaders in storycentric communities are timeless and universal. They contain lessons that are applicable from generation to generation across the globe.

These universal principles tend to take on diverse forms and methods. There is not just one *way* to lead like Jesus. Christ-centered leadership in a storycentric community can vary in style depending on factors such as the cultural context, the appropriate leadership "type," and follower experience.

CULTURAL CONTEXT

A community's culture affects the values of its members. For instance, some cultures are time-oriented while others are event-oriented, and this influences much of their activity. People in the Majority World have often told me, "You have watches, we have time." Both perspectives, in balance, can be faithful to Scripture, and the leader's style needs to adjust accordingly.

Another cultural difference that significantly impacts leadership is how "power distance" is perceived. People in cultures where the distance between leaders and followers is high are more comfortable with leaders who take charge. This also typically occurs in societies that are more status-oriented than achievement-oriented. In other words, a greater value is placed on power that has been inherited or otherwise granted, as opposed to that which has been achieved solely by merit. People in status-oriented cultures tend to be more secure with leaders who employ a more directive style—albeit still within the framework of "leading with a towel."

Furthermore, many storycentric cultures prioritize the group above the individual. Whereas Westerners are often enculturated to stand up for themselves and to choose their own path, people in many other parts of the world act predominantly as members of a cohesive group. Communication occurs in groups, learning is done through groups, and group dialogue is crucial for creating understanding among the members. "Koinonia" or "community" comes naturally in such cultures, particularly in those that are more storycentric. Christ-centered leadership in group-oriented cultures rightly focus more on developing the group rather than singling out individuals within the group. In a more individualistic culture, the Christ-centered leader properly focuses more on the highest potential of individuals.[1]

LEADER "TYPE"

The "type" of leader needed also impacts the application of Christ-centered leadership principles. For example, someone who leads a house church will express the leadership principles of Jesus differently from a denominational head. While both should be committed to influence and potential rather than power and control, the application of Christ-centered leadership will be manifested in different ways.

To distinguish various expressions of Christ-centered leadership, it has been helpful to classify leaders into five types: (1) This type leads a small group of people with direct, face-to-face influence as he or she guides and encourages; (2) This type supervises other volunteers in their local area; (3) This type serves full-time in a local ministry, such as a pastor, local mission leader, or church planter.

Their influence is broader because they have more time to devote to the task; (4) This type has a regional focus, perhaps as the district mission director or the principal of a Bible college; and (5) This type has national or even international responsibilities as policy-maker, conference speaker, or leader of a multinational ministry.

Two things must be noted with regard to the above classification. First, the application of Christ-centered leadership principles is expressed differently in each of these types. For example, the small group leader needs to relate to people at a more intimate level than an international conference speaker. Second, classifying leadership by type is not intended to view the roles as hierarchical in nature, but rather to demonstrate the importance of each. Each type of leader is crucial for the growth and development of ministries, and each requires a different approach for effective, Christ-centered leadership.[2]

FOLLOWER EXPERIENCE

Christ-centered leaders must also adjust their style of leadership to the needs of the individuals they lead. For example, a person who is new to a job function will need more directive leadership, whereas someone who is already capable in their ministry role will function best with a delegation style of leadership.

Situational Leadership Theory asserts that there is no single "best" style of leadership. Effective leadership is task-relevant and relationship-focused, with the most effective leaders being those who adapt their leadership style to the task maturity level or the confidence level of the individual or group.

Sometimes it is best to "tell" a novice what needs to be done. Someone who is a "rookie" on a job may be enthusiastic and willing to work on the task, but they are not yet competent enough to take responsibility on their own. At other times, it is better to "sell" the idea. That is, the leader provides most of the direction, but uses two-way communication and provides the support that will allow the individual or group being influenced to buy into the process.

For followers who are more experienced but lack confidence in a task, leaders can use a "participating" approach, sharing decision-making on how to proceed with the task while maintaining close relationships. And for those followers who are both experienced and confident in their task ability, the leader can use a "delegating" approach, passing on both the task and the responsibility to the group or individual while the leader stays involved to monitor progress.

No single style is considered optimal for all leaders to use all the time; each can be part and parcel of their portfolio. To be truly effective, Christ-centered leaders should be flexible and willing to adapt themselves according to the situation, to optimize their followers' highest potential.[3]

SNAPSHOTS

What image comes to mind when you hear the term "Christ-centered leadership"?

- A robed priest?
- A bearded philosopher?
- A business professional?
- An admiral?
- A strict parent?
- A person who looks a lot like you?

Here are a few snapshots of Christ-centered leaders who serve in storycentric communities in various parts of the world:

- Raj's vision and values have their origin and resolutions in the story of the community to which he belongs.
- Sue orchestrates, communicates, and influences rather than relying on command and control.
- Carlos empowers people with authority, resources, information, and accountability to be the best they can be.
- Millie publicly defends those who stand for what is true and right.
- Pho champions sound moral behavior as a sufficient end in itself.

- Yam models that collaboration serves the interest and well-being of all involved.
- Karina is openly accountable for her decisions.
- Andrew prioritizes the continued personal growth and well-being of others.
- Francoise displays conviction and willpower, but insists that followers not allow her will to replace their own.
- Manori provides an environment that is safe enough for people to take a risk, and sometimes even to fail in their risking.
- Antonia creates an atmosphere where people are free to tell the truth in constructive ways, especially to the leaders.
- Hwa encourages people to tell their own stories.
- Trevor treats each person with sacred respect because they are uniquely crafted in the image of their Creator.
- Robin champions people to pursue their God-given dreams.
- Andrea shares credit, and celebrates others' accomplishments.

These are just a few examples. Neither the Scriptures nor this book provides an exhaustive list of descriptors for Christ-centered ministry leaders in the twenty-first century; but the leadership that Jesus modeled and taught forms the cornerstone. It is a kind that focuses on a long-view perspective, prioritizes virtue, pursues authentic relationships, and sees and develops the potential of others. Regardless of a leader's other competencies, it is only possible to lead like the "King with a towel" by living out these principles.

LET'S SEIZE THE MOMENT

People's trust in institutions and their leadership has seriously declined in the new millennium. Organized religion, government bureaucracy, business executives, media bias, and financial institutions have eroded public confidence. The Tea Party and Occupy movements in America and the Arab Spring in the Middle East are recent expressions in which millions have voiced confusion and anger toward leaders and the institutions they represent.

Yet, in the midst of the chaos, even the more cynical admit that things would be different if they could just have healthier leaders. As Kouzes and Posner observe in *The Leadership Challenge*, "Younger workers aren't giving in to the idea that they don't make a difference. Aging baby boomers are back to exploring their souls. More and more of us are on a quest for greater meaning in our lives."[4]

Although younger generations are increasingly absent from the church, many haven't abandoned their faith. They are merely looking for effective Christ-centered leaders who will listen to the dreams that God has birthed in them rather than force-feeding yet another ministry program. They want help solving the messy problems of life and discovering a vital faith for the workplace. They seek leaders who are absolutely convinced that Jesus reigns supreme when His people are developed and released to run on all cylinders.

It's time for a leadership reformation. The older generation must take the first steps to earn back the trust that has been lost, and then take further steps to sustain it. While Christ-centered leadership does not always guarantee Christ-centered followers, it does establish the tone, set the stage, and offer options. To foster hope for the future, there must be a commitment from leaders.

As noted earlier, such a reformation won't be easy. Christ-centered leaders may in fact, like the faithful ones before them, experience the pain most intensely. As they strive to clarify meaning, unify people, and intensify actions, they may feel the uneasy tension between releasing and constraining people's choices. The more effective leaders will be those who learn to embrace the contradictions—for where there is tension, there is also truth. And where there is truth, there is the chance for progress. As they navigate these tensions and a host of other forces, seen and unseen, the leaders must make sure that their followers have the opportunity to discuss, debate, and reconcile as necessary.

Liberating as this way of leadership is, it doesn't happen on its own. While we may strongly desire to be this kind of leader, we often find ourselves unable to do so—at least, with any consistency. In those times when we're unable or unwilling to "lead with the towel," when we find ourselves in situations where Jesus' way of leadership just doesn't make sense, it usually means that it's time for us to let Him wash our feet again. It's time for us to let our Servant-King—who knew where He had come from and where He was going, who knew that He was in the absolute center of His Father's will, and whose heart overflowed with love—minister to us afresh. To the degree that we let Him love and serve us, to the degree that we allow Him to heal and help us, to that degree will we wash the feet of those we have been entrusted to lead.

CHAPTER 12 SUMMARY

- Christ-centered leadership in a storycentric generation can vary according to one's context.
- Factors that create variations in the way Christ-leadership looks include cultural context, appropriate leadership "type," and follower experience.
- Snapshots of Christ-centered leadership are provided from storycentric contexts around the world.
- A leadership reformation can occur as ministry leaders surrender to Jesus Christ, and allow Him to wash their feet again.

PART FOUR

The Garden Project

THE GARDEN PROJECT: OUR JOURNEY

The ministry of Freedom to Lead International (FTL) was launched in 2009 to fill a critical need for Christ-centered leaders in storycentric communities. FTL began to provide a leadership development program in India and Nepal for the Bridges Training Network of South Asia, a consortium of eighteen storycentric church planting ministries. The program is called *The Garden Project*. This initiative has now expanded into various nations throughout eastern and western Africa.

The following pages will give a glimpse into the work that Freedom to Lead has been doing to develop Christ-centered leaders in a storycentric generation. Hopefully *The Garden Project* will inspire readers to dream of a movement that will impact storycentric communities all across the globe.

FTL's Emphasis

Four categories of leadership development were described in chapter five: character formation, biblical literacy, context-specific skills, and ministry development. FTL offers leadership development for storycentric leaders primarily in two of these categories: character formation and ministry development. More precisely, we aim to cultivate leaders who will be able to integrate Christ-like character with the disciplines necessary to develop a ministry.

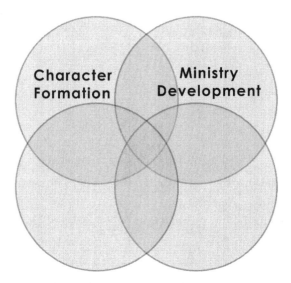

Freedom to Lead International

Ministry leaders need help integrating their spiritual convictions with effective organizational principles and practices that are genuinely Christ-centered. Many say that ministry development has been overlooked in their development, an omission that has resulted in their seeking help from sources not compatible with their Christian commitment. For example, secular resources on the topic of Leading Change work on the assumption that organizational success is the leader's ultimate goal; therefore, getting rid of those slow to embrace change is expected and encouraged. Unfortunately, many Christian leaders have applied these lessons and only later realized that their ministries are not consistent with Paul's instructions to the Thessalonians when he said, "Warn those who are idle, encourage the timid, help the weak, be patient with everyone" (1 Thess 5:14). FTL's program seeks to bridge this gap between character formation and ministry development.

The Garden Project provides some context-specific skills, and the principles we advocate are based on the authority of the Bible. However, we cannot provide all that an emerging Christ-centered leader needs, so we are committed to partnering with other leadership development service providers that specialize in developing *biblical literacy* and *context-specific skills* for storycentric leaders.

The task of cultivating Christ-centered servants to lead the church in the twenty-first century is extremely challenging, and we are aware that FTL is not the be-all and end-all of leadership development. FTL needs partners who address the categories that we don't. We need each other, for we are all parts of a whole. That's what being the body of Christ is all about—not just among church members, but also among those of us who provide leadership development in the name of Jesus Christ.

FTL's Competencies

Before developing the curriculum and launching the program, FTL spent a year conducting in-depth interviews with ministry leaders and their followers in Africa, Asia, North America, and South America. The interviews were intended to ascertain the competencies related to character formation and ministry development deemed necessary for Christ-centered leadership in storycentric communities. After many interviews, a handful of core competencies surfaced that are common to each of these ministry contexts. These competencies became FTL's primary focus in our work with emerging leaders in storycentric communities.

We desire to see the Lord raise up leaders who:

1. Demonstrate and cultivate character

Christ-centered leaders are spiritual leaders. They demonstrate integrity through their personal and public behavior. They emphasize growth and learning for themselves and those they influence. They champion people and standards that embody core biblical values.

2. Model authentic relationships

Christ-centered leaders treat others with respect, forgiveness, and acceptance. They lead out of humility, honesty, and love. They teach and practice healthy relationships.

3. Inspire a shared vision
Christ-centered leaders communicate a compelling image of a preferred future. They motivate others to envision and act toward worthy possibilities.

4. Challenge people and processes
Christ-centered leaders practice innovative ways to improve themselves and the people they lead. They experiment and take risks to release individuals to reach their highest kingdom potential.

5. Craft a healthy ministry culture
Christ-centered leaders align the ministry's values with biblical values. They steward resources so that the ministry is self-sustaining and self-propagating. They facilitate decisions and lead change in a collaborative environment.

6. Facilitate interpersonal and organizational communication
Christ-centered leaders foster an environment where people are safe to tell the truth. They model and teach peacemaking and people management skills.

7. Implement strategic planning
Christ-centered leaders build capable teams and partnerships that discern and respond to God's initiatives with clear goals and effective strategies to accomplish a clear, common, and compelling mission.

8. Consider the individual
Christ-centered leaders understand and value the individuals they lead. They tailor their leadership approach to others' cultural, gender, and personal needs.

9. Develop people
Christ-centered leaders intentionally develop others. They assist those they influence to identify and use their gifts. They challenge and support others in their development.

10. Advance cooperative partnerships
Christ-centered leaders conduct their lives and ministries under the Lordship of Christ, in partnership with His Spirit, and in cooperation with other kingdom-minded people and ministries.

FTL's Sources

Freedom to Lead relies on three primary sources to inform these Christ-centered leadership competencies: the examples and teachings of Jesus in the Gospels; complementary biblical lessons; and culturally appropriate stories, images, and music.

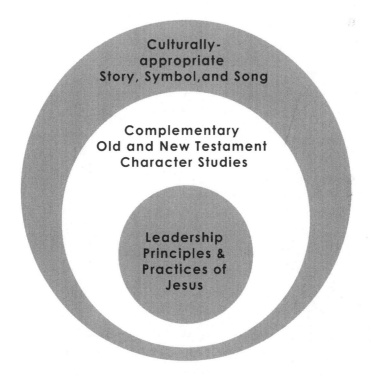

The core leadership principles of *The Garden Project* begin with the example and teaching of Jesus. In storycentric contexts, we employ Gospel stories, images, music, and drama that highlight Jesus' leadership principles and practices as the primary guide for Christ-centered leadership. Other narratives from both Testaments as well as poems and proverbs are used to complement the core Christ-centered principles. We also rely on culturally appropriate storycentric arts that support these biblical principles and practices. In storycentric communities, it is imperative to differentiate clearly between biblical stories and cultural stories, since the learners have very limited access to the source text and may rely solely on what they hear.

FTL's Strategy

FTL applies a ministry strategy that employs three integrated process steps: module presentation; mentoring; and module transference.

1. Module Presentation

First, FTL presents the following intensive modules to a select group of participants:

Leadership for a Healthy Ministry: This module exposes the unhealthy leadership behaviors, beliefs, and worldview that are hindering the quality and growth of churches and ministries. A leadership approach that uses people to serve the leader's agenda is compared to a Christ-centered leadership approach that cultivates people and trusts God for the results. Selected gospel narratives reveal Jesus' leadership priorities that included meeting people's deepest needs, cultivating others to reach their highest potential, and calling His followers to serve others as He had served them.

Strategic Leadership: This module builds upon *Leadership for a Healthy Ministry* to construct a ministry strategy. Key elements include: (1) developing a strategy with the whole Gospel in mind, (2) cultivating people as a strategic component of healthy ministry, and (3) identifying mission. The module highlights three tools that leaders can use to prioritize cultivating people while executing mission: (a) modeling and teaching, (b) allocating resources, and (c) rewarding behavior that advances the ministry's mission and values.

Mentoring: Although the term "mentoring" does not appear in the Bible, principles and practices of mentoring can be observed in Jesus' ministry as he prepared the disciples for their future leadership. This module advocates and applies three essential mentoring principles. First, effective mentoring is based upon a relationship between mentor and mentee. Second, mentors who listen responsibly and ask good questions foster self-discovery learning for the mentee. Third, mentees benefit most from mentors who share their own story with authenticity.

Peacemaking:[1] Christ-centered leaders are called to be peacemakers who demonstrate God's commitment to redeem conflict. This module presents biblical illustrations to understand how one's own story fits into God's ultimate plan of redemption. Principles of peacemaking are reviewed, and competencies for crafting a culture of peace are learned. The peacemaking leader represents God's continuing redemptive cycle of confession, forgiveness, and renewal in the world today.

Leading Change: The unfolding drama of redemption is a story of continual change; therefore, guiding God's people through change is a fundamental competency for Christ-centered leaders. This module equips leaders to understand and navigate the sense of loss that people experience as they encounter change. In light of the typical resistance to needed change, principles for leading individuals and collectives through the change process are taught and applied.

Leading Teams, Coordinating Partnerships: Based on the Holy Trinity's model of teamwork, this module teaches that serving together within ministries and across ministries (partnerships) has potential for growth toward deeper Christian maturity and greater kingdom impact. Key competencies including mission, roles, facilitation, and decision-making are applied to lead teams and coordinate partnerships.

Spiritual Leadership: Christ-centered leaders need an intentional strategy to cultivate their own spiritual growth and the spiritual lives of others. This module emphasizes the foundational principle that spiritual life and growth result from the dynamic interplay of God's faithfulness and our obedience. Based on this principle, five "streams" of Christ-centered spiritual growth from the Scriptures and subsequent history are taught and applied: (1) the new life, (2) the abiding life, (3) the empowered life, (4) the compassionate life, and (5) the witnessing life.

Stewardship and Sustainability:[3] Followers of Jesus Christ are entrusted by God to steward what He owns. This module teaches ministry leaders to steward local resources toward the fulfillment of Jesus' final command to be his witnesses locally and beyond (Acts 1:8). Empowering and mobilizing the local church is a critical factor for long-term ministry sustainability.

. . .

The leadership principles in each of these modules are taught through biblical and cultural stories. The primary teaching method is storytelling followed by discussing strategic questions related to the stories, questions that emphasize the key leadership principles to be learned. The stories are supplemented by relevant images, and are brought to life by original indigenous music and drama that reinforces the leadership principles.

Several module samples of *The Garden Project* are available online at freedomtolead.net. These samples provide glimpses into what we have worked out to this point in the crucible of field-testing, and address questions such as: What does leadership training for storycentric learners look like? How do we effectively highlight the Christ-centered leadership principles outlined in this book among those who learn best through stories, symbols, drama, and song?

2. Mentoring

Second, FTL provides each participant with mentoring, which we have found is popular and powerful in storycentric communities. The mentors provide needed support to the participants during the grind of their challenging leadership responsibilities. They give timely, personalized feedback by asking probing questions like: What went well in this leadership situation? If you could do this leadership task over again, what would you do differently? Questions such as these lead to self-discovery, which leads to improved leadership skills. The mentoring approach establishes relationship as the foundation for influencing the participants and it has proved very effective among adults in storycentric cultures.

3. Module Transference

Third, each participant transfers the modules and the mentoring to another group of participants within his or her network. FTL's mission is to impact some of the most under-resourced areas of the world with leadership development. By providing guidance as participants teach and mentor their own network of leaders, these Christ-centered leadership principles are penetrating into areas that otherwise cannot be reached due to the limitations of language, culture, and geography.

LESSONS LEARNED

As we navigate these uncharted waters, we are lifting experimental sails. We are often tossed to and fro by the unpredictable winds of trial and error, but our craft is making headway. The following are some of the primary lessons we have learned to date.

1. Effective storycentric communication is far more than just telling stories to highlight deeper leadership principles; it requires consistent patience to allow the story to communicate the lessons intended. As one who has had many years of education that emphasizes bulleted lists of abstract thought, I am constantly challenged to trust that the story itself will communicate the message.

The FTL team was once teaching around thirty Muslim-background believers in Ethiopia. All participants could read and all were also storycentric learners, so during the training sessions we told biblical stories and relevant fictional stories that communicate Christ-centered leadership principles. Later, during the Q&A session, the participants were engaged and quickly got the point as long as the discussion was within the framework of the story. Questions like "In the story where Jesus called Simon to fish for people, how did Jesus inspire Simon?" generated enthusiastic and insightful responses. On the other hand, questions like "What lessons do *you* learn from this story?" consistently elicited blank stares followed by silence. These leaders assume that the story embodies the truth for themselves, so they tend to interpret explicit application as confrontational and offensive.

2. In telling biblical accounts, great care should be taken not to embellish or otherwise "craft" the story. Since storycentric learners tend to rely on verbal transmission of information from person to person rather than a source text, fidelity to the inspired Scriptures is supremely important.

3. The details of fictional stories are also essential when teaching storycentric learners. In book cultures, the narration of a story tends to be condensed and approximate since the original is recorded in writing. For example, if I am retelling a story to Western friends, I'll often say, "The story goes something like this." I will skip familiar details and restrict myself to only those aspects that I need to highlight. In storycentric cultures, however, the survival of the story depends on verbal accuracy. Learners in these cultures attend carefully to—and even enjoy—the details, and they expect greater precision in the storytelling process.

4. Repetition is essential in storycentric learning. Although it tends to annoy literacy-based learners (who are tempted to think or say, "I've heard that already!"), storycentric learners need and expect repetition of lessons for better retention.

5. Storycentric communication is most effective when it is formatted simply for ease of learning, but we must bear in mind that *simple* and *simplistic* are not the same! While storycentric people do not easily grasp abstract, theoretical points, their deep ruminations are unleashed through tangible images, relatable stories, and music that is familiar to their ear.

6. As the FTL team has sought to communicate with story-centric learners, our most significant "aha" moments have typically occurred when the participants transfer the modules to another

generation of participants. Many storycentric learners are from cultures where critique is regarded as offensive, so rather than directly tell us how to improve, they *show* us. As we observe them teach the modules to others, we discover how to communicate more effectively. Such opportunities have afforded us invaluable times of steep learning.

An Example from India

The Garden Project is one way to address the challenge of cultivating storycentric leaders. We know it is not the only way, and we look forward to the day when others build on these initial efforts to provide reliable mapping for impact among the emerging generation of leaders and their ministries.

Deepak lives with his wife and children in North India, an area of the world where persecution against Christian believers has been severe. His own story of radical conversion to Christ from Hinduism can testify to this. He is educated and has some biblical training, and he wants to use the experiences and abilities God has given him to grow the church. With a passion to reach his own people in a way that truly speaks to them, Deepak has served God faithfully by planting churches in storycentric communities. The network of churches and ministries he now coordinates in these communities has experienced rapid growth, and the opportunity before him continues to be vast. But there was a time when Deepak couldn't help becoming frustrated and fatigued due to the lack of resources available to him, especially as he watched storycentric community churches begin to close.

As this happened, Deepak began to see that faithful, competent leadership is not only needed, but it is crucial for planting and cultivating healthy churches in communities like his. So he began praying for the necessary growth opportunity for the leaders in his network. God answered Deepak in a very specific way: by introducing him to *The Garden Project.*

Deepak has been a participant of *The Garden Project* for several years, and is now using the program throughout his network. This is how he describes the impact FTL's storycentric leadership development initiative has had on his region:

> I just thank God for Freedom to Lead, which came to us at the right time. To be honest, we did not know where we were heading with church planting after receiving a greater and wider response from the community. When we first became part of *The Garden Project*, our idea of leadership was different. Before then, top-down leadership was our understanding, but over these past few years all that has changed. We are now better equipped to face challenges as our network works together. A big thank you to God. May He bless and use *The Garden Project* mightily to help and build other Christian leaders. This is our prayer.

While we still have a lot to learn, *The Garden Project*'s integrated strategy of module presentation, on-the-job mentoring, and module transference is transforming the lives of many participants. We continually hear testimonials that remind us about the importance of developing Christ-centered leaders who will unleash the power of the whole gospel in their communities. Stories like Deepak's give us reason to hope and greatly rejoice.

Leaders do make a huge difference in people's lives. The task of cultivating the emerging generation of Christ-centered leaders in storycentric communities is therefore crucial. Communities that are influenced most through stories, images, drama, and song need leaders who are not shackled by the kind of unhealthy leadership models that use people to amass power for the leader's success. Instead, they need leaders who engender trust as they value and build those they lead.

We regularly ask participants in our workshops to identify the leader who has influenced their lives most. Our goal for this exercise is twofold: we hope they will discover for themselves what it takes to have an influence on others; and we want them to discover that within each of them lies the power to make a difference.

Virtually everyone we have asked has been able to name at least one leader whose influence they have personally felt. On the rare occasion it's a well-known figure—perhaps someone from the past who changed the course of their nation's history. Or it may be a contemporary role model who serves as an example of effective leadership—a corporate head or athlete, for instance. Most often, however, it's a leader who is personally close to them—a parent, friend, pastor, teacher, or coach. The person is neither famous nor incredibly successful by conventional standards, but his or her influence on the participant is unmistakable. Such examples accentuate the truth that ordinary leaders are having an extraordinary impact.

This simple exercise spotlights leaders whose skills, styles, and contexts may vary widely, but who consistently display unusual character in the trenches of everyday living. When faced with tough choices, they often lead with a long-view perspective. They are motivated to invest in others with unyielding faith in a better future. They are women and men of notable virtue—not because they are perfect, but because they are unwavering in their commitment to live and lead biblically. Without exception, these leaders give of themselves to see others rise to their highest potential. And they do so without expecting the favor in return. Rather, they urge those they bless to pass on the blessing to another spiritual generation. In summary, these leaders collectively reflect the Christ-centered leadership lessons that are described in this book.

These storycentric leaders debunk the destructive myth that leadership is reserved for only an elite few. They demonstrate that leadership is not a position, a special gene, or a secret code. They dispel the notion that the only real leaders are the ones with the capital L at the top of the ladder. They dismiss the false perception that only the lucky ones can ever understand and apply the intricacies of effective leadership.

So let's do away with the myth. Rather than viewing leadership as a mystical mantle that we either have or don't have, let's begin to invest our time and energy into men and women with the belief that they can and will develop to become effective, Christ-centered leaders. Let's sow the seed with hope that God will bring the growth.

The call for leadership development is an urgent one, but despite the urgency, it is important to remember that developing leaders takes time. We should take a cautious stance toward the idea that leadership development can be "fast-tracked." For example, it often takes two or three years to learn optimally from an on-the-job assignment, in order that the emerging leader experience the consequences of decisions made and actions taken. It takes time to dig beneath the symptoms to understand the core challenges that a rising leader faces. And changing leadership behavior does not happen overnight, since it requires repeated feedback and ongoing practice. Because developing a leader takes time, we need to begin now.

God is birthing a brigade of ordinary people in storycentric communities to become extraordinary kingdom servants. Nobody said it would be easy; their quest for excellence may always seem to be just over the horizon. But the kind of leadership we've been talking about is attainable with concentrated effort and the energizing work of the Holy Spirit. These emerging leaders will need to keep growing in character and in biblical understanding. They'll have to hone skills that are specific to their ministry role, whether they work in the church or among unreached people. And learning to develop their ministry organizations in ways that honor Jesus Christ is a must. With sufficient desire and motivation, solid training, caring mentoring, and challenging on-the-job assignments, they can develop the thinking, values, and skills necessary to be the leaders God wants them to be.

We are living in what may be the most exciting era in church history. Unprecedented opportunities abound to expand the kingdom of God, and the church of Jesus Christ is advancing despite opposing social, cultural, and spiritual forces. Storycentric learners make up a majority of the world's people. So let's not lose another moment to start raising up the next Christ-centered leaders, equipping and empowering them to lead their storycentric generation into the fullness of our Lord Jesus Christ.

ENDNOTES

Introduction

1 Many names throughout the book have been changed.
2 Grant Lovejoy, National Assessment of Adult Literacy NAAL, "The Extent of Orality," *Orality Journal* 1 (2003): 11–39.
3 Mission CEO Survey 2013. Missio Nexus, 2013.

Part 1: Storycentric Learning

Chapter 1: The Power of Story

1 Fred Craddock, *Preaching as Storytelling* [Audio CD set] (Marietta, GA: Bell Tower Productions, 1981).
2 Kendall Haven, *Story Proof: The Science Behind the Starting Power of Story* (Westport, CT: Libraries Unlimited, 2007), 7.
3 Jay Winsten, "The Designated Driver Campaign: Why It Worked," *Huff Post Media Blog* (March 18, 2010).
4 Alan Deutschman, *Change or Die: The Three Keys to Change at Work and In Life*, New York, NY: HarperBusiness, 2005, 4.
5 Richard Daft, *The Leadership Experience*. Independence, KY: Cengage Learning, 2014.

Chapter 2: Literacy and Story

1 John Harlow, "Gutenberg, Man of the Millennium," *Time Magazine* 154 (1999): 14.
2 Jean Drèze and Amartya Sen, *An Uncertain Glory: India and Its Contradictions* (Princeton, NJ: Princeton University Press, 2013), 163.
3 Iain McGilchrist, *The Master and His Emissary: The Divided Brain and the Making of the Western World* (New Haven, CT: Yale University Press, 2010), 4.

4 Mike Metzger, *Doggie Head Tilt Blog*. Retrieved from http://www .doggieheadtilt.com.

5 McGilchrist, *The Master and His Emissary*.

6 Shane Hipps, *Flickering Pixels: How Technology Shapes Your Faith* (Grand Rapids: Zondervan, 2009), 40.

7 Marshall McLuhan, *The Gutenberg Galaxy: The Making of Typographic Man*, Toronto, University of Toronto Press, 1962, 41.

8 Hipps, *Flickering Pixels*, 47

9 Ibid., 48.

10 Ibid., 49.

11 C. S. Lewis, *The Weight of Glory* and other Addresses (New York: Harper and Collins, 2009), 26.

12 John Piper, *Desiring God: Meditations of a Christian Hedonist* (Colorado Springs: Multnomah, 2003), 18.

13 Lesslie Newbigin, *Proper Confidence: Faith, Doubt, and Certainty in Christian Discipleship* (Grand Rapids: Eerdmans, 1995), 33.

14 Grant Lovejoy, National Assessment of Adult Literacy NAAL, "The Extent of Orality," *Orality Journal* 1 (2003): 11–39.

15 Donald A. Carson, *The Gagging of God* (Grand Rapids: Zondervan, 1996).

16 Metzger, *Doggie Head Tilt Blog*.

17 ION/LCWE, *Making Disciples of Oral Learners* (Lima, NY: Elim Publishers, 2005), 69.

18 Conversation with Kwotua in Accra, Ghana in the Fall of 2009.

19 W. Hamilton, *Phaedrus and the Seventh and Eighth Letters* (Hammondsworth, UK: Penguin Books, 1973), 96.

20 Neil Postman, *Technopoly: The Surrender of Culture to Technology* (New York: Vintage Books, 1993), 5.

21 NCTE Committee on Storytelling. *Teaching Storytelling: A Position Statement from the Committee on Storytelling of the National Council of Teachers of English* (Urbana, IL, 1992).

22 Haven, *Story Proof*, 4.

Chapter 3: Story As a Guide to Life

1 Haven, *Story Proof*, 4.

2 Roger Schank, *Tell Me a Story: Narrative and Intelligence* (Evanston, IL: Northwestern University Press, 1995), 10.

3 Jerome Bruner, *Making Stories: Law, Literature, Life* (Cambridge, MA: Harvard University Press, 2003).

4 Mark Turner, *The Literary Mind: The Origins of Thought and Language* (New York: Oxford University Press, 1996).

5 Haven, *Story Proof*, 4.

6 Jerome Bruner, *Acts of Meaning* (Cambridge, MA: Harvard University Press, 1990).

7 "The Science of Audience Participation." Lecture by Dr. Kathy Maxwell, Associate Professor of Biblical and Theological Studies at Palm Beach Atlantic University on April 8, 2015.

8 William B. Muster, *Time on Target: The World War II Memoir of William R. Buster* (Lexington, KY: University Press of Kentucky, 2015), 77.

9 Tom Wright, *The New Testament and the People of God* (Minneapolis: Fortress, 1992), 38.

10 International Orality Network (ION) and the Lausanne Committee for World Evangelization (LCWE), *Making Disciples of Oral Learners* (Lima, NY: Elim Publishers, 2005), 26.

Part 2: Leadership Development

Chapter 4: In Search of Leadership

1 Thomas Carlyle, *On Heroes, Hero-Worship, and the Heroic in History* (1840 lecture series delivered in London), edited by David R. Sorensen and Brent E. Kinser. New Haven, CT: Yale University Press, 2013.

2 Ralph M. Stogdill, "Personal Factors Associated with Leadership: A Survey of the Literature," *Journal of Psychology* 25 (1948): 35–71.

3 R. D. Mann, "A Review of the Relationship Between Personality and Performance in Small Groups," *Psychological Bulletin* 56 (1959): 241–70.

4 Jim Kouzes and Barry Posner, *The Leadership Challenge*, 3rd ed. (San Francisco: Jossey Bass, 2002), 386.

5 Paul D. Stanley and J. Robert Clinton, *Connecting: The Mentoring Relationships You Need to Succeed in Life* (Colorado Springs: NavPress, 1992), 18.

6 Peacemaker Ministries, *The Leadership Opportunity: Living Out the Gospel where Conflict and Leadership Intersect* (2009), 8.

7 David Bennett, *Future Leadership*, Lausanne Occasional Paper #41 (Lausanne Congress for World Evangelization, 2004), 3.

8 Author's Personal Conversation with Maia Mikhaluk.

Chapter 5: The Scope of Leadership Development

1 Adapted from "Our View of Leadership Development," by Ellen Van Velsor, C. McCauley, and R. Moxley, *Handbook of Leadership Development* (San Francisco: Jossey Bass, 1998), 1–3.

2 James M. Burns, *Leadership* (New York: Harper and Row, 1978). Also see A. Zaleznik, "The Leadership Gap," *Washington Quarterly* 6 (1983): 32–39

3 Composed by Bishop Ken Untener of Saginaw, drafted for a homily by Cardinal John Dearden in Nov. 1979 for a celebration of departed priests.

Chapter 6: The Process of Leadership Development

1 Jay Conger and B. Benjamin, *Building Leaders: How Successful Companies Develop the Next Generation* (San Francisco: Jossey-Bass, 1999), xi.

2 Stanley and Clinton, *Connecting: The Mentoring Relationships You Need to Succeed in Life.*

3 The PhD dissertation project researched 100-plus senior and midlevel leaders of a global Christian ministry. The leaders who participated in the study were from five continents: Africa, Asia, Europe, North America, and South America. Each leader was given a written description of the types of leadership development experiences outlined above. They were asked to indicate the type(s) of leadership development they had experienced in the past. Then each leader submitted to a 360-degree leadership evaluation. The tool employed in this feedback was Kouzes and Posner's Leadership Practices Inventory (LPI). This instrument scores a leader in five categories: (1) challenging the process, (2) inspiring a shared vision, (3) enabling others to act, (4) modeling the way, and (5) encouraging the heart. Each leader used the LPI to complete a self-evaluation, and the leader invited his or her supervisor, one person who reports to him or her (wherever applicable), and at least two peer coworkers to evaluate the leader by filling out the LPI. Based on this feedback, each leader was assigned an LPI score that reflected his or her current leadership effectiveness.

With this data, leaders were grouped according to the type(s) of leadership development they had experienced. Then the LPI scores of leaders were compared according to group. This dissertation research is available at:

Richard W. Sessoms, "The Relationship of Leadership Development Experiences to Kouzes and Posner's Five Practices of Exemplary Leaders," *The Leadership Challenge: A Wiley Brand*, March 30, 2014. http://www.leadershipchallenge.com/Research-section-Others-Research-Detail/abstract-sessoms-the-relationship-of-leadership-development-experiences.aspx

Part 3: Christ-Centered Leadership

Chapter 7: Leadership Matters

1 Robert Greenleaf, *Servant Leadership: A Journey into the Nature of Legitimate Power and Greatness*. Mahwah, NJ: Paulist Press, 1977.

2 George Barna, *Revolution* (Carol Stream, IL: Tyndale House, 2005).

3 Mike Metzger, *Sequencing: Will Your Company be Innovative over the Long Haul?* (Waukesha, WI: Game Changer Books, 2010).

4 Ibid.

5 Matthew B. Crawford, *Shop Class as Soulcraft: An Inquiry Into the Value of Work* (New York: Penguin, 2009), 42.

6 Marvin Weisbord, *Productive Workplaces: Dignity, Meaning, and Community in the 21st Century*, 25th Anniversary Edition (San Francisco: Jossey-Bass, 2012), 24-27.

7 William J. Mares and John Simmons, *Working Together* (New York: Knopf, 1983), 26.

8 Charles Murray, *Coming Apart: The State of White America, 1960-2010* (New York: Crown Publishing Group, 2012)

9 David Kinnaman, *You Lost Me: Why Young Christians are Leaving Church . . . and Rethinking* (Grand Rapids: Baker, 2011).

10 Douglas McGregor, *The Human Side of Enterprise* (New York: McGraw Hill, 1960).

11 Story adapted from The *Lengthening Shadow of a Great Man*, case study in course entitled "Making Human Strength Productive" (Colorado Springs, CO: Development Associates International, 2003), unpublished.

12 Liz Wiseman, *Multipliers: How the Best Leaders Make Everyone Smarter* (New York: HarperCollins, 2010), 4.

Chapter 8: Leadership Reformation

1   Sermon by Darrell W. Johnson entitled "The King Whose Scepter is a Towel," published by Preaching Today, Tape #90, © 1991.

2   Ibid.

Chapter 9: Leading with a Long View

1   Roger Parrott, *The Longview: Lasting Strategies for Rising Leaders* (Colorado Springs, CO: David C. Cook, 2010), 9.

2   Carpus and Papylus, in *The Early Christians in their Own Words,* ed. Eberhard Arnold (Farmington, PA: Plough, 1997), 73–75.

3   Speech at Peoria, Illinois, October 16, 1954. Recorded in *Illinois Journal,* October 1854.

4   Allen Guelzo, *Lincoln's Emancipation Proclamation: The End of Slavery in America* (New York: Simon & Schuster, 2004), 5.

5   The native inhabitants of Alaska were treated poorly in the years subsequent to Seward's purchase; therefore, this unfortunate outcome of U.S. expansion is noteworthy.

6   Doris Kearns Goodwin, *Team of Rivals: The Political Genius of Abraham Lincoln* (New York: Simon and Schuster, 2005).

7   Arthur Parker, *Sadhu Sundar Singh: Called of God* (London: Fleming H. Revell, 1920), 28–29.

8   Story adapted from Eric Metaxas, *Bonhoeffer: Pastor, Martyr, Prophet, Spy. A Righteous Gentile vs. The Third Reich* (Nashville: Thomas Nelson, 2010), 1-4.

9   Dietrich Bonhoeffer, *The Cost of Discipleship* (New York: Touchstone, 1937), 12.

Chapter 10: Leading with Virtue

1   Leighton Ford, *Transforming Leadership: Jesus' Way of Creating Vision, Shaping Values & Empowering Change* (Downers Grove, IL: InterVarsity, 1991).

2   J. Robert Clinton, *Focused Lives* (Altadena, CA: Barnabas Publishers, 1995), 499–500.

3   John Dickson, *Humilitas: A Lost Key to Life, Love, and Leadership* (Grand Rapids: Zondervan, 2011).

4   Joseph A. Michelli, *The Zappos Experience: Five Principles to Inspire, Engage, and WOW* (New York: McGraw Hill, 2012).

5   Adam Grant, *Give and Take: A Revolutionary Approach to Success* (New York: Penguin, 2013).

6   Drea Zigarmi et al., *Developing Leadership and Character: Knowing Enough About Yourself to Lead Others* (Escondido, CA: Zigarmi Associates, 2000).

7   Carl Jung, *Man and His Symbols* (Garden City, NY: Doubleday, 1964).

8   Erich Fromm. AZQuotes.com, Wind and Fly LTD, 2016. http://www.azquotes.com/author/5198-Erich_Fromm, accessed May 12, 2016.

9   Walter Isaacson, *Steve Jobs* (New York: Simon & Schuster, 2011), 117-124.

Chapter 11: Leading Others Toward Their Potential

1   James M. Kouzes and Barry Z. Posner, *The Leadership Challenge: How to Make Extraordinary Things Happen in Organizations* (San Francisco: Jossey-Bass, 2007).

2   Henri Nouwen, *In the Name of Jesus: Reflections on Christian Leadership* (New York: Crossroads, 1989).

3   Jim Collins, *Good to Great And the Social Sectors* (Boulder, CO: Jim Collins, 2005), 13.

4   Jim Collins interview with Francis Hesselbein, conducted when composing the foreword to *Hesselbein on Leadership* (San Francisco, CA: Jossey Bass, 2002), xi-xviii.

Chapter 12: Christ-centered Leadership Applied

1   See also Geert Hofstede, *Culture and Organizations: Software of the Mind* (New York: McGraw Hill, 1990).

2   Edgar Elliston, *Missiological Education for the 21st Century* (Maryknoll, NY: Orbis, 1996).

3   Paul Hersey and Ken Blanchard, *Management of Organizational Behavior – Utilizing Human Resources* (Upper Saddle River, NJ: Prentice-Hall, 1977), 172.

4   Jim Kouzes and Barry Posner, *The Leadership Challenge*, xxii.

Part 4: The Garden Project

Chapter 13: The Garden Project: Our Journey

1 FTL adapted the Peacemaking module from an earlier version written in collaboration with Dr. Karl Dortzbach of Peacemaker Ministries.

2 FTL adapted the Partnership module from curriculum originally created by visionSynergy called "Tree of Life".

3 FTL developed the Stewardship and Sustainability module in collaboration with International Steward.

REFERENCES

Barna, G. 2005. *Revolution*. Carol Stream, IL: Tyndale House.

Bennett, D. 2004. *Future Leadership*. Lausanne Occasional Paper #41. Lausanne Congress for World Evangelization.

Bonhoeffer, D. 1937. *The Cost of Discipleship*. New York: Touchstone.

Bruner, J. 1990. *Acts of Meaning*. Cambridge, MA: Harvard University Press.

———. 2003. *Making Stories: Law, Literature, Life*. Cambridge, MA: Harvard University Press.

Burns, J. 1978. *Leadership*. New York: Harper and Row.

Carlyle, Thomas. (1840 lecture series delivered in London), *On Heroes, Hero-Worship, and the Heroic in History*, edited by David R. Sorensen and Brent E. Kinser. New Haven, CT: Yale University Press, 2013.

Carpus and Papylus. The Early Christians in their Own Words, ed. Eberhard Arnold (Farmington, PA: Plough, 1997), 73–75.

Carson, D. A. 1996. *The Gagging of God*. Grand Rapids: Zondervan.

Clinton, J. R. 1995. *Focused Lives*. Altadena, CA: Barnabas Publishers.

Collins, J. 2005. *Good to Great And the Social Sectors*. Boulder, CO: Jim Collins.

Conger, J., and B. Benjamin. 1999. *Building Leaders: How Successful Companies Develop the Next Generation*. San Francisco: Jossey-Bass.

Craddock, F. 1981. *Preaching as Storytelling* [Audio CD set]. Marietta, GA: Bell Tower Productions.

Crawford, M. 2009. *Shop Class as Soulcraft: An Inquiry Into the Value of Work*. New York: Penguin.

Daft, R. 2014. *The Leadership Experience*. Independence, KY: Cengage Learning.

Deutschman, A. 2005. *Change or Die: The Three Keys to Change at Work and In Life*. New York, NY: HarperBusiness.

Dickson, J. 2011. *Humilitas: A Lost Key to Life, Love, and Leadership*. Grand Rapids: Zondervan.

Drèze J., and A. Sen. 2013. *An Uncertain Glory: India and Its Contradictions*. Princeton, NJ: Princeton University Press.

Elliston, E. 1996. *Missiological Education for the 21st Century*. Maryknoll, NY: Orbis.

Ford, L. 1991. *Transforming Leadership: Jesus' Way of Creating Vision, Shaping Values & Empowering Change*. Downers Grove, IL: InterVarsity.

Fromm, E. AZQuotes.com, Wind and Fly LTD, 2016. http://www.azquotes.com/author/5198-Erich_Fromm, accessed May 12, 2016.

Goodwin, D. K. 2005. *Team of Rivals: The Political Genius of Abraham Lincoln* (New York: Simon and Schuster).

Grant, A. 2013. *Give and Take: A Revolutionary Approach to Success*. New York: Penguin.

Greenleaf, R. 1977. *Servant Leadership: A Journey into the Nature of Legitimate Power and Greatness*. Mahwah, NJ: Paulist Press.

Guelzo, A. 2004. *Lincoln's Emancipation Proclamation: The End of Slavery in America*. New York: Simon & Schuster.

Hamilton, W. 1973. *Phaedrus and the Seventh and Eighth Letters*. Hammondsworth, UK: Penguin Books.

Harlow, J. 1999. Gutenberg, man of the millennium. *Time Magazine* 154: 14.

Haven, K. 2007. *Story Proof: The Science Behind the Starting Power of Story*. Westport, CT: Libraries Unlimited.

Hersey, P., and K. Blanchard. 1977. *Management of Organizational Behavior–Utilizing Human Resources*. Upper Saddle River, NJ: Prentice-Hall.

Hipps, S. 2009. *Flickering Pixels: How Technology Shapes Your Faith*. Grand Rapids: Zondervan.

Hofstede, G. 1990. *Culture and Organizations: Software of the Mind*. New York: McGraw Hill.

International Orality Network (ION) and the Lausanne Committee for World Evangelization (LCWE). 2005. *Making Disciples of Oral Learners*. Lima, NY: Elim Publishers.

Isaacson, W. 2011. *Steve Jobs*. New York: Simon & Schuster.

Jung, C. G. 1964. *Man and His Symbols*. Garden City, NY: Doubleday.

Kinnaman, D. 2011. *You Lost Me: Why Young Christians are Leaving Church . . . and Rethinking*. Grand Rapids: Baker.

Kouzes, J, and B. Posner. 2002. *The Leadership Challenge*. 3rd ed. San Francisco: Jossey Bass.

Lewis, C. S. 1941. *The Weight of Glory*. (New York: Harper and Collins, 2009), 26.

Mann, R. D. 1959. A review of the relationship between personality and performance in small groups. *Psychological Bulletin* 56: 241–70.

Mares, W. J., and J. Simmons. 1983. *Working Together*. New York: Knopf Doubleday.

Maxwell, K. "The Science of Audience Participation." Lecture, Palm Beach Atlantic University on April 8, 2015.

McGilchrist, I. 2010. *The Master and His Emissary: The Divided Brain and the Making of the Western World*. New Haven, CT: Yale University Press.

McGregor, D. 1960. *The Human Side of Enterprise*. New York: McGraw Hill.

McLuhan, M. 1962. *The Gutenberg Galaxy: The Making of Typographic Man*. Toronto, University of Toronto Press.

Metaxas, E. 2010. *Bonhoeffer: Pastor, Martyr, Prophet, Spy. A Righteous Gentile vs. The Third Reich*. Nashville: Thomas Nelson.

Metzger, M. *Doggie Head Tilt Blog*. Retrieved from http://www.doggieheadtilt.com.ed.

———. 2010. *Sequencing: Will Your Company be Innovative over the Long Haul?* Waukesha, WI: Game Changer Books.

Michelli, J. A. 2012. *The Zappos Experience: Five Principles to Inspire, Engage, and WOW*. New York: McGraw Hill.

Murray, C. 2012. *Coming Apart: The State of White America, 1960-2010* (New York: Crown Publishing Group).

Muster, William B. 2015. *Time on Target: The World War II Memoir of William R. Buster* (Lexington, KY: University Press of Kentucky.

Newbigin, L. 1995. *Proper Confidence: Faith, Doubt, and Certainty in Christian Discipleship*. Grand Rapids: Eerdmans.

Nouwen, H. 1989. *In the Name of Jesus: Reflections on Christian Leadership*. New York: Crossroads.

Parker, A. 1920. *Sadhu Sundar Singh: Called of God*. London: Fleming H. Revell.

Parrott, R. 2009. *The Longview: Lasting Strategies for Rising Leaders*. Colorado Springs, CO: David C. Cook.

Piper, J. 2003. *Desiring God: Meditations of a Christian Hedonist*. Colorado Springs: Multnomah.

Postman, N. 1993. *Technopoly: The Surrender of Culture to Technology*. New York: Vintage Books.

Schank, R. 1995. *Tell Me a Story: Narrative and Intelligence*. Evanston, IL: Northwestern University Press.

Stanley, P. D., and J. Robert Clinton. 1992. *Connecting: The Mentoring Relationships You Need to Succeed in Life*. Colorado Springs: NavPress.

Stogdill, R. M. 1948. Personal factors associated with leadership: A survey of the literature. *Journal of Psychology* 25: 35–71.

Turner, M. 1996. *The Literary Mind: The Origins of Thought and Language*. New York: Oxford University Press.

Van Velsor, E., C. McCauley, and R. Moxley. 1998. *Handbook of Leadership Development*. San Francisco: Jossey Bass.

Weisbord, M. 2012. *Productive Workplaces: Dignity, Meaning, and Community in the 21st Century*. 25th Anniversary Edition. San Francisco: Jossey-Bass.

Winsten, J. 2010. The Designated Driver Campaign: Why it Worked. *Huff Post Media Blog* (March 18).

Wiseman, L. 2010. *Multipliers: How the Best Leaders Make Everyone Smarter*. New York: HarperCollins.

Wright, Tom. 1992. *The New Testament and the People of God*. Minneapolis: Fortress.

Zaleznik, A. 1990. "The Leadership Gap," *Washington Quarterly* 6.

Zigarmi D., K. Blanchard, M. O'Connor, and C. Edeburn. 2000. *Developing Leadership and Character: Knowing Enough About Yourself to Lead Others*. Escondido, CA: Zigarmi Associates.

N

Nazareth, 29, 148
Nazis, Nazism, 163, 182
new covenant, 144–46, 153
Newbigin, Lesslie, 25
Nietzsche, 20
Noland, Chuck, 170
North America, 18, 127, 215

O

occupy movements, 207
O'Connor, Flannery, 36
old covenant, 144–45
one-eyed prophets, 28–29
Ornish, Dean, 14

P

Palestine, 144, 148
Papylus, 157–59, 164
partnerships, 216–17, 219
peacemaking, 79–80, 216, 219
Piper, John, 25
Plato, 113
political voice, 17, 33
Posner, Barry, 55, 208
Postman, Neil, 29
Pot, Pol, 113
power
    steward of, 193
    legitimate use of, 193
    destructive use of, 194–96
prudence, 171, 175–79, 185–86

Q

quality of life, 16, 18, 33

R

Rabbi Heschel, 113–14
Reality Field Distortion (RFD),
    183–84
Reformation, 141, 143, 153, 182,
    208–09
    Reformers, 17
Reid, John, 99
Rice, Condoleezza, 100
Rockefeller, John D., 124
role models, 62, 69, 180
    lack of, 62, 69, 180
Roman Catholic Church, 17, 168
Russia, 124, 160

S

Santali tribe, 7–8
Satan, 68, 156
    devil, 157–58
    worship, 68
Saturation Church Planting, 127
Saxe, John Godfrey, 81
Schank, Roger, 36
Schurz, Carl, 161
Scientific Management, 58,
    122–23, 129, 133
    theory, 133, 141
    Taylorism, 122, 124–25
Sen, Amartya, 16
Serbia, 121
Seward, William, 160–61, 164
Sikh, 161
Singapore, 18
Singh, Sadhu Sundar, 161–62, 164
skepticism, 8, 191, 201
Social Security, 17, 33
Socrates, 29
South America, 17, 215